D1321425

THE SAILING COMPANION

Miles Kendall

A THINK BOOK FOR

PORTICO

It isn't that life ashore is distasteful to me.
But life at sea is better.

Sir Francis Drake

A Think Book
for Anova Books

First published in Great Britain in 2004
This edition published in 2008 by
Portico
10 Southcombe Street, London W14 0RA

Reprinted in 2008

An imprint of Anova Books Company Ltd

Edited by Miles Kendall
The Companion team: Tilly Boulter, James Collins, Rhiannon Guy,
Emma Jones, Jo Swinnerton, Lou Millward Tait
and Malcolm Tait

Think Publishing
The Pall Mall Deposit
124–128 Barlby Road, London W10 7BL
www.thinkpublishing.co.uk

ISBN 9781861058393

Printed and bound by WS Bookwell, Finland

www.anovabooks.com

We who adventure upon the sea, however humbly, cannot but feel we are more fortunate than ordinary people.

Claud Worth

IT'S ALL BEEN PLAIN SAILING BECAUSE OF...

my father and mother who gave me a love of the sea, and my wife, who gave me a son to pass that love on to.

And thanks to
Judy Darley, Felicity Egerton, Selina Erham, Nicola Haynes, Lois Lee, Nancy Waters

There is a magic to the sea. It draws us to it and holds us in its thrall. We want to make our homes beside it, swim in it, holiday by it shores. It is a living thing, never still. Its mood can change from calm and peaceful to violent and deadly within minutes. It can erode headlands or give birth to new islands. And to venture out to sea under sail is the greatest thrill of all.

The romance of sailing is undeniable. Gliding through the water, the wind in your hair and the sun on your face is as good as it gets – though it isn't always so blissful. When there's a gale blowing and your crewmates are bent over the side, bidding farewell to their lunch, things may not seem so rosy. But that's the beauty of going to sea – you never know quite what to expect. There is always a new lesson to be learnt or a new delight to be experienced.

There are plenty of publications that explain how to sail – but this is not one of them. Instead it is an eclectic collection of nautical knowledge. It seeks to cast some light on why people cast off their lines and set course for somewhere beyond the horizon. I hope that it will also remind us that sailing is something that shouldn't be taken too seriously. There exists a great body of writing on sailing – this is just a drop in the ocean.

Miles Kendall, Editor

DOING ANYTHING NICE
FOR YOUR HOLIDAYS?

Fancy a week away from it all on a yacht? What about soaking up the Mediterranean sunshine or escaping the European winter for rum and fun in the Caribbean? In that case, why not charter Mirabella V, the largest single-masted yacht in the world.

Launched in 2004, Mirabella V is an awe-inspiring 246ft 8in long and almost 50ft wide. Her masts stands 292ft high, which prevents her from passing under the Golden Gate Bridge. A massive hydraulic lifting ram can raise the keel from 33ft to a mere 13ft.

Owner Joe Vittoria made his fortune when he sold the Avis car rental empire but still needs to charter her out to cover the bills and $50 million building costs. The $250,000 weekly rate may seem steep, but that's not the end of it. 'Parking' Mirabella V for the night can set you back about $2,000 – and then there's the pilot's fees, food, drinks and fuel. A 10% tip is considered the minimum, meaning that the bill for your week in the sun is likely to exceed $335,000.

So what do you get for your money? A 600-bottle wine cellar, two swimming pools (one fresh water, one salt) and a crew of 11, but only 12 berths for you and your friends. Book now to avoid disappointment.

QUOTES ON BOATS

I can't wait for the oil wells to run dry, for the last gob of black, sticky muck to come oozing out of some remote well. Then the glory of sail will return.
Tristan Jones, yachtsman

THE REALITY OF SAILING

Smells

Take six people who can only bring limited changes of clothes on board and place them in the close confines of a yacht. Make them wear thick clothing and rubber boots. Add regular physical exercise to work up a sweat. Ensure the limited supply of water combined with the cramped confines of the heads or shower make them unwilling to wash. Prevent any airflow through the cabin by keeping hatches closed in case waves break over the boat. Feed them on bacon butties, beer and curry. Install a tiny toilet with yards of piping in which pongs can fester. It's no wonder that yachtsmen head for the showers before the bar after a few days at sea.

10 *Millilitres of toothache solution carried by Chay Blyth on his non-stop circumnavigation of the world in 1970–71*

SAINTS FOR SEAFARERS

If you're in peril at sea, if no one else can help you, and if you can raise them on VHF, then maybe you can call for the help of the patron saints of seafarers, sailors, mariners, boatmen and watermen.

Saint	Memorial day
Anthony of Padua	13 June
Barbara	4 December
Botulph	17 June
Brendan the Navigator	16 May
Brigid of Ireland	1 February
Christina of Bolsena	24 July
Christopher	25 July
Clement I	23 November
Cuthbert	20 March
Erasmus	2 June
Eulalia	12 February
Francis of Paola	2 April
Jodocus	13 December
John Roche	30 August
Julian the Hospitaller	12 February
Michael the Archangel	29 September
Nicholas of Myra	6 December
Nicholas of Tolentino	10 September
Our Lady, Star of the Sea	Multiple days
Our Lady of Mount Carmel	16 July
Peter Gonzales	14 April
Phocas the Gardener	23 July
Walburga	25 February

WORDS ON THE WATER

Conversations sank to discussions of 'spotty botties' – a common ailment when our skins were always damp and salty – and to wondering how many times Tony's nose could peel without running out of skin. Poor Tony had a nose which peeled in the sun, out of the sun and, he was to discover, in the freezing cold as well. We examined our feet every day for 'Blue Feet Disease'. An affliction caused by buying a not inexpensive pair of deck shoes and actually wearing them on deck in the wet, not an unusual place to wear a deck shoe, one might think, but obviously not a place the manufacturers had designed them for. I spent many happy hours composing an imaginary letter of complaint and even tried to photograph my bright blue feet.

Clare Francis, *Come Wind or Weather*

Jonah thanked the whale and sat down with a sigh. He was glad to be alive but aware that he smelled strongly of plankton.

THOSE SEVEN SEAS IN FULL

Useful for people who like pub quizzes.
Second only to being able to name all seven dwarfs.

Arctic
Antarctic
North Atlantic
South Atlantic
Indian
North Pacific
South Pacific

PEES AT SEA

Toilets on boats – or heads, as they are properly called – are generally cramped and often malodorous affairs. If the vessel is heeled over or pitching through the waves, one is likely to emerge relieved but battered. How much nicer to let it all hang out in the open air and top up the sea directly – and that is what most yachtsmen do when away from the crowds. Such *al fresco* urination is not without its risks. Standing on the gunwhale, leaning overboard, one hand for the boat and one for the old chap, you put yourself in a precarious position. Many a sailor's corpse has been dragged from the water with the fly undone. So if you do pee at sea, make sure you hold on tight, and always have your back to the wind.

SAILING TERMS THAT
CONFUSE LANDLUBBERS

Weigh anchor

Anchors are, by and large, fairly heavy. It is one of their great assets when it comes to stopping a boat from drifting away. One's choice of anchor is dictated by two things: weight and design. There is a bewildering range of designs now available. In the olden days anchors looked like the ones you still occasionally see on tattoos, but that has all changed. You can now have a plough, a fortress or a Danforth at the end of your chain – and they all come in a variety of weights. However if asked to 'weigh anchor' you should refrain from getting the scales out. You are being requested to pull the anchor up from the seabed – though you will get a fair idea of how much it weighs in the process.

NAUTICAL PUZZLES

An impoverished yachtsman arrives at a fuel pontoon with a five-litre container and asks the attendant to put four litres of diesel into it. Unfortunately, the pump is broken and the only measure the fuel man has is a three-litre jug. How can the men measure out exactly four litres of diesel using just these two containers?

Answer on page 153

THINGS THAT GO MOO IN THE NIGHT

Night watches can be long and lonely affairs. It is easy for your mind to wander when you're huddled in the cockpit with one eye on the compass and one scanning the horizon for other ships. Many yachtsmen have experienced nocturnal visitors of different shapes and sizes. Some hear strange animal sounds – cats, dogs, pigs and even cows – others recognise human voices among the gurgle of the wake and whistle of the rigging.

Seafarers also talk of seeing strange things in the night. Some are simple illusions – a coiled rope becomes a sleeping snake; others properly hallucinate and see things that are not there at all. Joshua Slocum, the pioneering American yachtsman, told of someone coming aboard his yacht at sea and taking the helm for several hours. Visitors have been seen standing at the bow and even on top of the mast. Indeed a study in 1972 found that half of the sailors who had crossed the Atlantic single-handed had experienced some type of illusion or hallucination. Solitude, sleeplessness and stress are the likely causes – though some still blame the mermaids.

It is not just the surface of the sea that is always moving – its level is constantly changing too. Depths of water and the heights of rocks and sandbanks on a chart are measured from a common level of tide known as the chart datum. This is also referred to as the Lowest Astronomical Tide as it is the lowest level to which the tide will fall due to any combination of astronomical conditions. It is very rare for the tide to ever drop this low, but cartographers are a naturally cautious lot.

Look at the areas of water on a chart and you will see a lot of numbers. These are depths or heights in metres and tenths of metres. An underlined number indicates a drying height of a feature that can be covered and uncovered by the tide. Thus an underlined number three shows an area of seabed that stands three metres above the level of chart datum. Were the number three not underlined, you would know that at the spot the sea was three metres deeper than the level of chart datum.

Tides are all added to chart datum. If there is a four-metre tide our three-metre rock will be a metre beneath the waves, while there will now be seven metres of water at the point that was three metres deep.

Tides are never constant and this complicates things even more. Spring tides are big tides: the water rises and falls more than average. These are the tides that reveal rarely seen wrecks and sandbanks. Neap tides are altogether more modest, rising and falling less than average.

A ready reckoning system helps sailors make sense of all this tidal trickery. Average heights of tide for both neaps and springs are given, so that you know what to expect. Mean High Water Springs (MHWS) is the average height of the highest high tides and is important to know, as it is the level from which the chartered heights of objects on land are measured. If a chart says that a lighthouse is 30 metres high, you know that it is 30 metres above MHWS. This is useful, as knowing how high an object is allows you to calculate how far you are from it.

Establishing what sort of tide, or height, or depth is being referred to can be a confusing process, yet it is child's play compared to actually working out how much water you will have under your keel at a certain place at a certain time. It is principally for this reason that many sailors have such a soft spot for the virtually tideless Mediterranean.

14 *Estimated height, in metres, of the largest waves encountered during a Force 12 hurricane*

BLACK STUFF AT THE BOAT SHOW

A curious thing happens to sailors at the annual London Boat Show. No matter what their tipple of choice is for the other 364 days of the year, everyone drinks Guinness. This strange phenomenon could be explained away if there were numerous young lovelies serving these old sea dogs their pints of stout, but nothing could be further from the truth. The same organised crew of middle-aged men are employed year after year to pull the pints, and pull them they do – some 57,000 a week. The Guinness stand is the universal rendezvous. If you turn up at the Boat Show alone, head here. Even if you've never been near a boat in your life you're bound to meet someone you know.

WORDS ON THE WATER

The master, the swabber, the boatswain and I,
The gunner and his mate
Loved Mall, Meg and Marian and Margery,
But none of us cared for Kate;
For she had a tongue with a tang,
Would cry to a sailor, Go hang!
She loved not the savour of tar nor of pitch,
Yet a tailor might scratch her where'er she did itch:
Then to sea, boys, and let her go hang!

William Shakespeare,
Stephano's song from *The Tempest*, Act II, scene ii

A NAUTICAL STORY

This true story recently appeared as a reader's confession in the pages of *Yachting Monthly*.

A family go for a sail on their yacht. They anchor off a remote beach and go ashore to explore. Mum and Dad climb through waist-high heather to the clifftop while their two boys play on the sand. On reaching the top, the parents see that the bigger of the boys has his brother on the ground and is pushing sand into his face. 'Stop that at once!' shouts the father, at which point a young couple emerge shocked and in a state of undress from the heather just a few yards from where the parents stand. Thinking that the order had been directed at them, the lovers hastily button themselves up while the parents, equally embarrassed, mutter an apology and head back to the beach as quickly as they can.

COOKING FAT

You don't have to spend too long wandering around a marina before coming across a catamaran with the name Cooking Fat inscribed proudly across her sterns. A strange name for a boat, you may think – until you transpose the initial letters.

TO THE MED THE EASY WAY

If you want to cruise the Med but don't fancy sailing out into the Atlantic and across the Bay of Biscay then why not meander through French rivers and canals? Starting from Le Havre the route is:

River Seine
River Yonne
Canal de Bourgogne
Tunnel to Dijon
River Saône
River Rhône
The Mediterranean

THE COST OF A HONEYCOMB SANDWICH

A strong boat used to mean a heavy boat, but the advent of new materials has made it possible to build boats that are both incredibly strong and light. Weight is kept to a minimum by combining an outer shell of a hard material with a filling of a lighter material. The technique is known as sandwich construction and glassfibre was first used as the bread and balsawood as the filling. When Kevlar and carbon composite materials became available to boat builders, a whole new world of possibilities opened up.

By combining outer layers of Kevlar and carbon with a foam filling, an immensely strong sandwich can be created and many modern racing hulls are made from such materials. One of the strongest and lightest sandwiches available to the modern designer is the honeycomb sandwich: cells of hi-tech Nomex paper, looking just like honeycomb, stand between out-layers of woven Kevlar creating a light but rigid structure.

These space-age materials are prohibitively expensive for all but the wealthiest yachtsmen and are rarely seen beyond the racing circuit. They also have their limitations. Team Philips, the catamaran that was meant to carry Pete Goss around the world, was built using huge amounts of honeycomb sandwich, but unfortunately went on to break apart in the Atlantic during a storm.

The sail, the play of its pulse so like our own lives: so thin and yet so full of life, so noiseless when it labours hardest, so noisy and impatient when least effective.
Henry David Thoreau, author and philosopher

SEEING THE LIGHT

Light signals at sea and how to tell them apart

Fixed (F):
This light is constantly on and shines with steady intensity.

Flashing (Fl)
The total duration of light is always less than the duration of the darkness.

Quick Flashing (Qk Fl)
The light flashes between 50 and 79 times per minute. The total duration of light is shorter than darkness.

Very Quick Flashing (V Qk Fl)
Between 80 and 159 flashes per minute, usually 100 or 120. The total duration of light is shorter than the darkness.

Interrupted Quick Flashing (I Qk Fl)
Like Quick Flashing, but with one moment of darkness in one period.

Group Flashing (Gp Fl)
A series of flashes followed by a period of darkness. A light which flashed three times would be shown as Gp Fl(3) on a British chart.

Long-Flashing (LFL)
This light has one long flash in a period. A long flash is at least two seconds long.

Isophase (Iso)
This light has equal duration between light and darkness. A period consists of both a light and a dark interval.

Occulting (Occ)
Occulting is the opposite of flashing – the light is more on than off. Can be Group-occulting or Composite Group-occulting.

Alternating (Alt)
An alternating light that changes colour. A light that flashes white and red would be marked Alt WR on a chart.

Morse (Mo)
A light showing a letter from the Morse code alphabet, replacing dots and dashes with flashes and long flashes. The letter 'U' would be shown as a light flashing the Morse for 'U' (- - —), would be recorded as Mo(U) on a chart and would show two flashes followed by a long flash.

Length, in feet, of the Exocet anti-ship missiles 17

CRUISING COCKTAILS

Sea breeze

Two types of sea breeze can be found at sea and both can serve the yachtsman well. The first occurs when the sun heats the land, causing the air above it to warm and rise. The cooler air over the sea is drawn onto the land to replace the heated air and an onshore sea breeze is created.

The second sort of sea breeze is also found on warm summer days but easier to create. Simply take two parts vodka, three parts cranberry juice and three parts grapefruit juice. Pour over ice into a highball glass. Garnish with a slice of lime. Recline in cockpit and enjoy.

CHARTING THE HEIGHTS

You can't find just any old building on an Admiralty chart. Only the following can become annotated landmarks:

Brick kiln	Institute	Refinery
Castle	Lattice tower	Sailor's home
Cathedral	Lookout station	School
Cement works	Machine house	Sewage works
Cold store	Mast	Spa hotel
Column	Monastery, convent	Structure
Electric works	Mooring mast	Telegraph office
Factory	Multi-storey building	Town hall
Floodlight	Naval college	Warehouse
Gas works	Navigation school	Water mill
Greenhouse	Office	Water works
Hotel	Observatory	Well
House	Power station	
Hut	Pyramid	

FOLKBOAT

She's old-fashioned and she's bang up-to-date. She's a gentleman's cruiser that is thrashed round the cans. She's a coastal potterer that has been sailed around the world. The Folkboat is full of surprises and contradictions. The result of a Scandinavian design competition, the Folkboat ended up being designed by committee after no one winner was selected. That was in 1941 and the first Folkboats came to the UK later that decade. It proved sea-kindly and exciting to race, and a class association was formed. Folkboats have been built in many countries and in many different ways since, and there are all sorts of variations on the Folkboat theme.

WORDS ON THE WATER

From the log of the barque Storm, Atlantic Ocean, south-east of Bermuda, October 22, 1854.

First part blowing heavy and an awful sea on. At 7pm while close reefing the main topsail was struck by a perfect hurricane. The foremast was struck by lightning from the royal yard down to the eyes of the lower rigging where the mast snapped and went over the side and the barque broached to and went over nearly on her beam ends, when the main top mast and mizzen topmast backstays were cut away and both masts went, the mainmast close to the deck and the mizzen in the eyes of the lower rigging. The barque righted and paid off with the wreck hanging under her stern and threatening every minute to knock the rudder off. With great exertions we finally cleared it without further damage. At this time it was blowing frightfully so that it was dangerous to expose ourselves to the force of the wind... After the wreck was cleared the barque behaved much better than I expected and shipped little water though wallowing badly.

Captain John P Roberts

QUOTES ON BOATS

We are monarchs of all we survey and owe allegiance to none but the weather.
Frank Cowper, yachtsman and author

DRAKE TIES THE KNOT

The point at which the homeward path of a round-the-world passage crosses the outward bound route is where a circumnavigator 'ties the knot' – and the first Englishman to do so was Sir Francis Drake. It is believed that Drake learned the ropes in the Thames coastal trade before going to sea properly, where he showed great aptitude and quickly rose up the ranks. In 1577 he was appointed to command the first English expedition to circumnavigate the globe. With five ships and some 160 men, he set sail from Plymouth on 13 December. The journey was full of incident, perhaps the most dramatic episode being the trial and beheading of Thomas Doughty, captain of one of the ships, on a charge of mutiny. Two of the smaller ships were sunk on purpose, another was separated from Drake's Golden Hind in a storm, and the remaining small sloop was lost at sea. Drake returned to England in 1580 and presented Queen Elizabeth with gold, silver and jewels taken from Spanish treasure ships he had raided off the Pacific Coast of Peru and Mexico.

FERRY NUFF

If you don't fancy hoisting sail yourself, you can always do it the easy way and get a ferry across the Channel. You'll be in good company, as legions of yachtsmen now keep their boats in France and commute to them by ferry.

From	To	Hours	Company
Plymouth	Santander	18	Brittany Ferries
Plymouth	Roscoff	6	Brittany Ferries
Poole	Cherbourg	4$1/4$	Brittany Ferries
Portsmouth	St Malo	9	Brittany Ferries
Portsmouth	Ouistreham	6	Brittany Ferries
Portsmouth	Le Havre	5$1/2$	P&O Ferries
Portsmouth	Bilbao	35	P&O Ferries
Portsmouth	Cherbourg	4$3/4$	P&O Ferries
Portsmouth	Cherbourg	2$3/4$ (cat*)	P&O Ferries
Portsmouth	Caen	3$1/2$	P&O Ferries
Newhaven	Dieppe	2 (cat*)	Hoverspeed
Newhaven	Dieppe	5	Transmanche
Dover	Calais	1 (cat*)	Hoverspeed
Dover	Calais	1$1/2$	Sea France
Dover	Calais	1$1/4$	P&O Ferries
Dover	Dunkirk	2	Norfolkline

(cat: catamaran service)

NAUTICAL PUZZLES

You are sailing along when your yacht hits something in the water. There is a hole in the side of the boat over which you must secure a 28in by 28in wooden board. You'll need to secure the board with 29 nails on each side of the square. Each nail must be at the same distance from the neighbouring nails.

How many nails will you need?

Answer on page 153

SEA SAYINGS

As the crow flies

Crows are not sea birds and will head for land by the most direct route (as the crow flies). When unsure of their position in coastal waters, ships would release a caged crow. The crow would fly upwards until it spied land and then head for the shore, giving the vessel some sort of a navigational fix. The best place to follow the crow's progress was from a platform near the top of the mast – the crow's nest.

QUOTES ON BOATS

There is nothing – absolutely nothing – half so much worth doing as simply messing about in boats.
Ratty, in Kenneth Grahame's *The Wind in the Willows*

THEY DON'T NAME THEM
LIKE THAT ANY MORE

Some Royal Navy ship names from the good old days

Indomitable (1907)
Inflexible (1907)
Invincible (1907; sunk 1916)
Superb (1907)
Indefatigable (1909; sunk 1916)
Thunderer (1911)
Audacious (1912)
Valiant (1914)
Courageous (1916)
Furious (1916)
Glorious (1916)
Renown (1916)
Repulse (1916; sunk 1941)

BLOW ME!

Sails can work in one of two ways. Imagine Tom Sawyer and Huckleberry Finn on their raft with a bed sheet rigged up as a sail and the wind exactly behind them, blowing them along. That simple pushing motion is how the most basic sails work and is how yachts are driven straight downwind by their giant, colourful spinnakers.

When the wind is not behind them, modern sails work more like the wings of an aeroplane. They are made so that they become curved when the wind blows over them. Some even have huge batons that keep them permanently curved. This shape creates greater pressure on the windward side of the sail than on the leeward (downwind) side. This pressure difference keeps a plane in the sky and drives a yacht through the water, helped by the shape of the hull.

Yachts were built with wings instead of sails in the late twentieth century, with mixed results, but the designers have not given up and the fastest sailing vessels on the planet being built today have solid, vertical wings instead of traditional sails.

Yachtsmen like to race. Some do so unofficially, tweaking their sails to try to catch up with the boat in front of them as they cruise down the coast. Others race only occasionally, taking part in an annual club event. And there are many sailors who take to the water only in order to compete.

If the racing is organised, and the fleet made up of different designs, then a handicapping system is needed to create a level playing field on which the yachts can compete with some kind of parity.

Handicapping is the way in which race committees attempt to allow slow boats to race against fast boats and declare which boat was sailed the best. That at least is the theory. The reality involves huge amounts of confusion, rule-bending, arguments, calculations and occasional skullduggery.

There are almost as many handicapping systems as there are international racing committees. Each one looks at the yachts that race in its events and adopts the system that works best. Yachts may be handicapped according to a complex set of calculations that take into consideration sail area, length, weight, hull shape and numerous other factors to produce a rating. The International Measurement System is one such system that has been widely adopted.

The problems start as soon as the formula is declared. Designers and victory-hungry sailors start to tear it apart, looking for loopholes that they can exploit. A few years later, yachts start to emerge from boatyards with exaggerated shapes. The stern may be very narrow, a huge bowsprit may have been added, odd attachments may have blossomed on keels.

All these changes are designed to make the boat go faster without affecting the handicap. If the designers are successful, there are only two options for the race committee. They can either accept the changes and thus oblige all the other skippers to copy them if they wish to remain competitive, or change the rules to outlaw the new designs. Whichever route they take, there will be a lot of unhappy yachtsmen.

Such wrangling is inevitable with any form of yacht handicapping system and sailors have got used to it. Those who wish to promote the sport have taken an alternative route. When all the yachts are the same there are no problems with handicapping. The first over the line is the winner. The public can understand what's going on and so are more likely to watch the action, and sponsors are therefore easier to attract. Sometimes the simplest solutions are the best.

22 *Number of 'outright' records recognised by the World Sailing Speed Record Council. The giant catamaran Playstation holds 13 of them*

The bowline

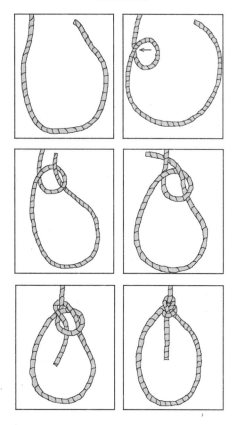

Take a long working end of a rope over the standing part to form a small loop. Hold the loop in place with one hand. Pass the working end through the loop from back to front. Take the working end behind the standing part. Now pass the working end up through the loop from front to back. Pull on the standing part and on the double working end to tighten the knot.

Alternatively: the rabbit goes up the hole, round the tree and back down the hole.

WORDS ON THE WATER

And the winds having fallen from us so that the Sayles did naught but hang without Life so that the Tackles swayed with the sway of our Shippe and the cordage set up a Moaning and a Crekeing that was over piteous: and in the Sky was not so much as even One Cloud nor yet a small Cloud and there was only the Sun which was sette there that Man should ever be beneath him. And those of Our Companie who were of the Sea they knew that it was of Small Avail to bewail and to cry and to shout for the Winds for these are of the Mighty God and His giving and do come to all men not of their asking but of His Gift. Then were we wont to sit about ourselves in the Great Cabin in two or in four or in many of us and make discourse of Seas and Divers Places and of Mountains and Strange Beastes and of the Good and the Evil of the case. Great store set we all by such Discourse in that when the Chance of the Day seemed ill with us yet we were in great part Content.

John Cartwright,
A Voyage to the South Indies

THE CURSE OF THE COCKROACH

Watch yachtsmen loading their boats with stores in sunny climes and you'll observe a strange ritual. Each item is taken out of the bag or box it was carried in and carefully inspected. Only once it has been certified 'cockroach free' is it passed below to be stowed away.

Ridding a yacht of cockroaches is a near impossible feat. Unlike houses, with their regular four-walled rooms, yachts are full of nooks and crannies where these wee beasties will hide away and breed. They come on board hidden among food and packaging, or, sneakiest of all, as eggs within cardboard boxes. Many sailors ban all cardboard for this very reason. Others soak bunches of bananas over the side for half an hour to ensure that all nasties swim away or drown.

If the worst does happen and the cockroaches get past your defences and set up home, then chemical warfare is one solution. Boric acid mixed with sugar should do the trick. Fumigation bombs are a more extreme option – open all lockers and drawers, throw in the bomb, close the hatches and leave the boat for a day. Another treatment will be required two weeks later to kill off any newly-hatched roaches.

A more environmentally-friendly solution comes with eight legs. Certain spiders, such as the Housekeepers found in the US, eat cockroaches for breakfast, lunch and dinner. Although this is not ideal for nautical arachnophobes, reportedly the spider keeps a very low profile once on board.

ALL DRESSED UP

Dressing overall is the yachting equivalent of putting on the glad rags and involves hoisting a string of flags from the bow, up to the top of the mast, then down to the stern. It is now common for all sorts flags to be flown in any order – but if you want to do it properly, then here's how:

E, Q, 3, G, 8, Z, 4, W, 6, P, 1, I, Code, T, Y,
B, X, 1st Sub, H, 3rd Sub, D, F, 2nd Sub, U, A,
O, M, R, 2, J, 0, N, 9, K, 7, V, 5, L, C, S.

WHAT A BLAST

Different vessels make different sounds in fog

Type of boat,
Sound signal (normally at least every two minutes)

Boats under 12m, *loud sound*

Powered vessel moving, *one long*

Powered vessel stopped but not anchored, *two long*

Tug, *one long, two short*

Vessel being towed, *one long, three short*

Sailing vessel, *one long, two short*

Vessels restricted in ability to manoeuvre
one long, two short

Trawler, *one long, two short*

Vessel aground, *three single strokes before
and after rapid ringing of the ship's bell*

Anchored vessel (less than 100m long),
rapid ringing of bell at least every minute

Anchored vessel (over 100m), *rapid ringing of bell,
followed by gong rung rapidly near stern*

A NAUTICAL JOKE

A yachtsman is sailing along when the boom knocks him on the head and he falls overboard. When he comes round, he's on a beach. The sand is dark red. He can't believe it. The sky is dark red. He walks around a bit and sees that there is dark red grass, dark red birds and dark red fruit on the dark red trees. He's shocked when he finds that his skin is starting to turn dark red too.

'Oh no!' he cries, 'I've been marooned!'

*Number of dollars, in billions, spent each year on marine leisure products 25
in the US*

Capturing the might and majesty of the ocean is difficult when confined to a studio lot at Pinewood or Hollywood. Waves just don't look right when they are created to float a model boat in a special-effects tank, though computer-generated animation is a big leap forward. Some directors even film at sea. Here are a few of the best sailing films.

Message in a Bottle
A sentimental affair with Kevin Costner as the owner of a pretty wooden sloop.

The Thomas Crown Affair
Not about sailing at all but contains thrilling footage of a catamaran race that culminates in a spectacular capsize.

Master and Commander
Slow-paced swashbuckler for the twenty-first century. The storm scenes are the most convincing to ever grace the silver screen.

The Perfect Storm
Several yachts are caught up in the vicious weather that decimates a North American fishing fleet. The stuff of nightmares.

The Riddle of the Sands
Michael York stars in this wonderfully dated adaptation of Erskine Childer's thriller. Great for lovers of wooden cruising yachts.

Waterworld
Ridiculous but watchable futuristic fable with Kevin Costner playing the seaman who starts to smell something fishy – himself.

Wind
Matthew Modine is the America's Cup skipper battling for national pride. Lots of sailing footage compensates for the implausible story.

The Old Man and the Sea
Hemingway's classic tale of the sea, wonderfully done for the big screen. Nominated for Oscars for Best Cinematography and Best Actor, and won an Oscar for Best Score.

SEA SAYINGS

Son of a gun

Sir Francis Drake once allowed a comely lass called Maria to sail on board the Golden Hind. Maria fell pregnant on board but the father of the child could have been anyone from the Captain down. Drake did the dishonourable thing and marooned her, for while taking women on board was common practice it was officially frowned open. If children were born aboard, as did happen, the delivery often took place between guns on the gun deck. If the child's father was unknown, they were entered in the ship's log as 'son of a gun'.

'Excuse me,' called Douglas, 'you don't have any water, do you? It's just that our canoe seems to be on fire.'

NAUTICAL PUZZLES

Which racing yachtswoman owned a boat whose politically incorrect name might have put her in a sticky situation?
Answer on page 153

TYPHOON WARNING

The Royal Hong Kong Yacht Club occupies a stunning site on the edge of one of the world's most famous harbours. The club has not moved its location, but yachtsmen who last visited in the first half of last century would not recognise it. The reason is that the club was originally built on an island and sailors would take small local boats, sampans, out to it. However, as Hong Kong prospered, land became a costly commodity and massive land reclamation projects were carried out to provide more land for sky-scrapers. Eventually Hong Kong's expanding shoreline reached the island and the sampan owners were out of a job.

They were not the only ones to regret the island's absorption. When typhoon warnings were issued in the past there would be a rush of yachtsmen out to the island, safe in the knowledge that within hours they would be trapped there, perhaps for days, with nothing to do but sit in the bar and get drunk.

WORDS ON THE WATER

By the end of the fourth day all his work was done, and on the fifth the goddess Calypso saw him off from the island. She bathed him first and dressed him in sweet smelling clothes. She had also stowed two skins in his boat, one full of dark wine, the other larger one of water, as well as a leather sack of grain and quantities of appetizing meats. And now a warm and gentle breeze sprang up on her command.

It was with a happy heart that the noble Odysseus spread his sail to catch the wind and skilfully kept the raft on course with the rudder. There he sat and never closed his eyes in sleep, but kept them on the Pleiads, or watched the late-setting Bootes slowly fade, or the Great Bear, sometimes called the Wain, which always wheels around in the same place and looks across at Orion the Hunter with a wary eye. It was this constellation, the only one which never sinks below the horizon to bathe in Ocean's Stream, that the wise goddess Calypso had told him to keep on his left hand as he sailed on his course, and on the eighteenth there came into view the shadowy mountains of the Phaecians' country, which jutted out to meet him. The land looked like a shield laid on the misty sea.

Homer, *The Odyssey*

QUOTES ON BOATS

Bad cooking is responsible for more trouble at sea than all other things put together.
Thomas Fleming Day, poet

MEET THE FLEET

The following are the boats of the Royal National Lifeboat Institution's fleet. All of them are paid for purely by voluntary donations.

Class	Length (m)	Crew	Top speed (knots)
Severn	17	6	25
Trent	14.2	6	25
Arun	16	6	18
Tyne	14.3	6	18
Mersey	11.7	6	17
Atlantic 75	7.3	3	32
Atlantic 21	6.9	3	29
D Class	4.9	3	20
E Class	9	3	20
Hovercraft	8.1	3	30

28 *Angle, in degrees, of a Boucher-style gunwhale on a traditional Greenland kayak*

SOME FACTS ABOUT SALT

The sea is made up of about 96.5% water and 3.5% dissolved salts. Salinity was once measured in parts per thousand but modern techniques now rely on electrical conductivity which gives rise to a number that indicates how salty a substance is.

The average salinity of the open ocean is around 35, although this can drop to as low as five where it is diluted by rivers, melting ice or very high rainfall. By contrast the water of the Red Sea can be as high as 40. The oceans are generally less salty around the poles, although there is also a band of low salinity around the equator. The North Atlantic is the saltiest large body of open ocean.

SAILING TERMS THAT CONFUSE LANDLUBBERS

Angel

Think 'angel' and you may conjure up images of cherubim and seraphim floating on clouds, idly stroking their harps. They will certainly be clean, white and airborne – unlike an angel on a boat, which is likely to be muddy, rusty, underwater and possibly made of lead. At sea, an angel is a weight attached to an anchor chain to make it more effective. Suspended halfway along its length, an angel helps ensure that the pull on the anchor is more horizontal than vertical. It also makes the motion of an anchored vessel more gentle and can limit her swinging circle.

RULE BRITANNIA!

Yacht racing became the sport of kings when, at the end of the nineteenth century, the royalty of Europe commissioned a series of stunning yachts in which to compete against one another. Most famous in home waters was Britannia, which was built for the Prince of Wales, later to become King Edward VII. Edward's nephew, Kaiser Wilhelm II, had bought a yacht of his own the previous year, and following Britannia's launch, he upgraded to the majestic cutter, Meteor.

Britannia was a spectacular vessel. She was 102ft long with a 110ft mast and 10,000 square-foot sail. It took more than a dozen men to hoist her mainsail. And she could sail. With a deep keel and powerful rig she was the fastest boat on the water and saw off competition from Europe and America. In fact, she was too fast. By taking the lion's share of silverware she prompted yacht clubs, designers and fellow competitors to rethink the regulations that governed the design of yachts to create a more level playing field.

There are six different types of buoy at sea and each is used for different purposes. As well as the shape of the buoy itself, further information can be gathered from the colour of the buoy and the shapes of any marks that are attached to it.

 1. CONICAL – looks like a pointed cone; typically used for unlit buoys to starboard.

 2. CAN/CYLINDRICAL – looks like a cylinder on end; typically used for unlit buoys to port.

 3. SPHERICAL – the part above the waterline is shaped like a sphere; typically used as unlit safe water or mid-channel buoys.

 4. PILLAR – typically a lattice tower mounted on a flat base; used just about anywhere, commonly as a base on which to mount a light.

 5. SPAR – in the form of a pole, or a long cylinder, floating upright; used just about anywhere, commonly with a light.

 6. BARREL – looks like a cylinder on its side; used only as a special mark.

WORDS ON THE WATER

Roll on, thou deep and dark blue Ocean – roll!
Ten thousand fleets sweep over thee in vain;
Man marks the earth with ruin – his control
Stops with the shore.

Lord Byron, *Childe Harold's Pilgrimage*

Land was created to provide a place for boats to visit.
Brooks Atkinson, American journalist

THE THINGS THAT ONLY SEAGULLS SEE

Taking to the high seas for pleasure is a relatively recent trend – little more than 150 years old. Nakedness has been around for much longer, of course, but has largely fallen out of favour in modern times. But many of today's yachtsmen buck the trend for wearing clothes and can often be found at the helm wearing nothing but a smile. Except, of course, that you can't find them, for that is joy of the ocean. There is so much sea out there that it is very easy to find a patch of it that is all your own and far from prying eyes. The curvature of the earth means that one has to venture only a few miles offshore before dipping beyond the horizon and into a private world where clothes are entirely optional.

Just imagine it. The burble of water beneath the bow, the wind in your hair and the sun on your skin – all of it. What could be more natural? After all, when did you last see a dolphin wearing Speedos?

For the long-distance yachtsman, nakedness is almost a necessity. Once clothes get wet with seawater they will never truly dry until rinsed in fresh water – a precious commodity. Having damp, salty clothes next to your skin spells trouble in the form of sores and boils. No clothes means no rubbing and no sores – problem solved.

Certain types of sailing vessel attract a higher level of nudity than others. Most famous are the Wharram catamarans. These twin-hulled boats come in a range of lengths and sizes (as do their owners) and designer James Wharram promotes a philosophy of cooperative construction and maximum nudity. He can regularly be found in the pages of the yachting press extolling the virtues of nakedness on board.

Nudity at sea is not without its problems. First, you must have good weather. No one enjoys fighting into the teeth of a sou'westerly gale in nothing but their birthday suit. Secondly, you must be in the right company – beware any yachts looking for crew if the skipper has a beard, an exceptional tan and a strange glint in his eye. Thirdly, you must take care of your behind. Sitting naked on a modern fibreglass boat encourages sweating and presents the risk of slipping overboard. A wooden boat will breathe beneath your buttocks but splinters are a constant hazard. Take off your clothes and take your pick.

ROPE SIZES

Next time you go down to the chandlery,
this is what you can order (in inches)

Diameter	Circumference
1/4	3/4
3/8	1 1/4
1/2	1 1/2
5/8	2
3/4	2 1/4
7/8	2 3/4
1	3

THE NATIONAL MARITIME MUSEUM, GREENWICH

The National Maritime Museum (NMM) was formally established by Act of Parliament in 1934 and opened to the public by King George VI on 27 April 1937. It includes the seventeenth-century Queen's House and, since the 1950s, the Royal Observatory. There is also a small museum at Cotehele Quay on the Tamar, Cornwall, with the NMM/National Trust sailing barge Shamrock, and the Valhalla ships' figurehead collection on Tresco, Isles of Scilly.

The collections comprise about 2.48 million items, many on loan to museums elsewhere in Britain. The public galleries at Greenwich display a selection and the remainder are accessible for public interest and research in various ways. From December 2002 the majority of the NMM smallboat collection has been on display at the new National Maritime Museum, Cornwall, in Falmouth.

The museum has the most important collection in the world recording the history of Britain at sea, including maritime art, cartography, manuscripts including official public records, ship models and plans, scientific and navigational instruments, timekeeping and astronomy (based at the Observatory). Its British portraits collection is exceeded in size only by the National Portrait Gallery, and its holdings related to Nelson and Cook, among many others, are unrivalled. The museum also boasts the world's largest maritime historical reference library (100,000 volumes), on whose shelves you can find books dating back to the fifteenth century.

The museum also holds great architectural importance: the Queen's House in particular is one of the keystones of the historic park-and-palace landscape of Maritime Greenwich, which was deemed a UNESCO World Heritage Site in 1997.

32 *Length, in feet, of the Nicholson 32 which 'began a revolution in building techniques', according to* Yachting World *magazine*

WORDS ON THE WATER

At midnight I was at the tiller and suddenly noticed a line of clear sky between the south and south-west. I called to the other men that the sky was clearing, and then a moment later I realised that what I had seen was not a rift in the clouds but the white crest of an enormous wave. During twenty-six years' experience of the ocean in all its moods I had not encountered a wave so gigantic. It was a mighty upheaval of the ocean, a thing quite apart from the big white-capped seas that had been our tireless enemies for many days. I shouted, 'For God's sake, hold on! It's got us!' Then came a moment of suspense that seemed drawn out into hours. White surged the foam of the breaking sea around us. We felt our boat lifted and flung forward like a cork in breaking surf. We were in a seething chaos of tortured water; but somehow the boat lived through it, half-full of water, sagging to the dead weight and shuddering under the blow. We baled with the energy of men fighting for life, flinging the water over the sides with every receptacle that came to our hands, and after ten minutes of uncertainty we felt the boat renew her life beneath us. She floated again and ceased to lurch drunkenly as though dazed by the attack of the sea. Earnestly we hoped that never again would we encounter such a wave.

Ernest Shackleton, *South*

WHAT LIES BENEATH

The colour of the sea is largely dictated by the nature of the seabed and how deep the water is. This simple rhyme offers practical advice to the uncertain sailor:

> *Brown brown, run aground,*
> *White white, you might,*
> *Green green, nice and clean,*
> *Blue blue, run right through*

CAPTAIN PUGWASH IS INNOCENT

It is widely but incorrectly believed that the Captain Pugwash cartoon, which was originally broadcast on the BBC between 1958 and 1967, featured characters including Master Bates, Seaman Staines and Roger the Cabin Boy. In fact, the crew on the Black Pig were called Master Mate and Tom the Cabin Boy, and fellow pirates were named Barnabas and Willy. John Ryan, Captain Pugwash's creator, won retractions and settlements from the *Sunday Correspondent* and *The Guardian* after both newspapers claimed that the show's characters had names worth sniggering over.

COASTAL CRUISING FIRST AID KIT

A few essentials for all eventualities

For common problems
Antacid tablets
Aspirin
Bandage
Peptic relief tablets
Provodine iodine
Thermometer (unbreakable)

Iodine
Razor, disposable
Roll gauze
Skin stapler, disposable
Skin staple remover
Synthetic gloves
Transparent wound covers

For minor trauma
Adhesive tape
Bandage
Bandage: fingertip
Bandage: knuckle
BZK antiseptic wipes
Gauze pads
Hydrogen peroxide
Paramedic shears
Triple antibiotic ointment
Tweezers with magnifier

For sprains and fractures
Adhesive tape
Splint (15in)
Elastic bandage
Finger splint
Ice bags
Ice tape
Safety pins
Triangle sling

Burns
Burn pads
Burn wraps
Sterile gauze

System problems
Alcohol prep pads
Calamine lotion
Cotton swabs
Elastic bandage
Eye wash and pads
Scalpel
Sting aid wand

For major lacerations
Adhesive tape
Benzoin swabs
Butterfly enclosures
Dressing pads
Gauze pads

CPR
CPR mask with valve
Oral airways device
Synthetic gloves

CRUISING COCKTAILS

Smooth Sailing

This long refreshing cocktail is popular with yachtsmen on the other side of the Pond. It slips down easily – very easily – so be careful that it is only the drink that ends up on the rocks.

To mix, take a good shot of vodka and add an equal amount of Triple Sec. Pour both over ice and top up with equal parts of orange juice and cranberry juice. If you own a motor boat or a humourously named yacht, you may wish to drizzle cherry brandy over the top.

---

34 *Number of years it took for a bible to be carried, onboard sailing vessels, thrice around the world. The bible was first given to Sir Robin Knox-Johnston*

WORDS ON THE WATER

In our sport, we have the man who sits in his study or office and forms his opinions by speculation; and the man who goes out on the water and gathers from experience facts upon which to base his ultimate findings. The many erroneous ideas regarding the design and handling of boats can be traced to the writings and talkings of the former type. And what is most strange, but seems to be true of all phases of human knowledge, such erroneous and some fatuous opinions find a wide and ready acceptance, whereas the real deductions of the experienced man are declined and derided.

Thomas Fleming Day, editor of *The Rudder* magazine

QUOTES ON BOATS

*Any damn fool can circumnavigate the world sober.
It takes a really good sailor to do it drunk.*
Francis Chichester, yachtsman

MAYDAY!

The word 'mayday' derives from the French phrase for 'Help me' – 'M'aidez'. A mayday call is the most urgent distress call that a vessel can broadcast and is used where a boat or person is threatened by grave and imminent danger and requires immediate assistance.

This is the mayday procedure recommended by *Reed's Nautical Almanac*:

- Check main battery switch is on
- Switch radio on, and select high power (25 watts)
- Select VHF Ch 16 (or 2182 kHz for MF)
- Press and hold down the transmit button, and say slowly and distinctly:
- 'Mayday, mayday, mayday'
- 'This is…' (name of boat, spoken three times)
- 'Mayday…' (name of boat spoken once)
- 'My position is…' (latitude and longitude, or true bearing and distance from a known point)
- Nature of distress (sinking, on fire, etc)
- Aid required (immediate assistance)
- Number of persons on board
- Any other important, helpful information (eg, if yacht is drifting, whether distress flares are being fired)
- 'Over'

On completion of the distress message, release the transmit button and listen.

I THINK I'LL BUILD MY BOAT WITH...

Ferro cement

Ferro cement arrived at around the same time as Glass Reinforced Plastic (GRP) but has not proved so successful. On paper it has a lot going for it: cheap, strong, durable, impervious to rot, rust, worms and osmosis – and it is easy to build with by yourself. It was this last 'advantage' that has crippled rather than created demand for Ferro cement boats. Many boats were built in back gardens across the length and breadth of the country. Some went on to sail the world, others never made it past the first stages of construction. Those that did were often incredibly heavy, due to liberal applications of Ferro cement. Home-builders frequently created huge hulls because the material was so cheap, then discovered that they could not afford the proportionately more expensive fixtures and fittings. Very few boats are built of Ferro cement these days.

THE GOLDEN GLOBE

Modern round-the-world racing started with the Golden Globe in 1968. The course was south from Falmouth, around the Cape of Good Hope at the tip of Africa, beneath Australia, across the Southern Ocean, round Cape Horn, up the Atlantic and back to Blighty. The winner, Robin Knox-Johnston, was the only man to complete the course and became the first person to circumnavigate the world single-handed and without stopping. The journey took him 313 days.

Of the eight other competitors, six didn't get beyond the Southern Atlantic. Chay Blyth was one of these but later made up for his disappointment by sailing non-stop around the world in the opposite direction – against prevailing winds and currents. The strangest tale is of Donald Crowhurst, a troubled man who had set to sea despite much self-doubt. Instead of sailing round the world, Crowhurst hid off the coast of South America until his competitors were on the final leg, at which point he re-emerged and joined the race, claiming to have rounded both Capes. The skipper of the vessel just ahead of him pushed his storm-battered yacht so hard that she broke up and he had to be rescued. Crowhurst was now likely to win the prize for the fastest passage. But he knew that his deceit was sure to be discovered and after leaving a rambling confession, he stepped overboard to his death.

The final entrant, Bernard Moitessier, did sail round the world but decided against returning to Europe and just kept going, passing south of Australia for a second time before putting in at Tahiti after 37,455 miles and 301 days at sea.

THE ALLURE OF BOATING

*Sandra's 'Introduction to Oarsmanship' classes had
proved popular with even the club's most experienced members.*

TYPES OF ANCHOR

Grapnel
Bruce
Delta
Fisherman
Danforth
Plough
CQR (secure – geddit?)

NAUTICAL PUZZLES

If you are the skipper, then it it all comes down to you;
you mustn't ever lose me, or the crew will lose theirs too.
What am I?
Answer on page 153

MAN OVERBOARD

Falling overboard from a yacht is always a life-threatening situation, but there are some simple precautions and techniques that can be adopted to maximise the chances of a safe recovery. It is now widely believed that furling the headsail and approaching the casualty under motor is the safest way to come alongside a MOB, but that is often just the start of the trouble. Lifelines at the stern of the boat should be secured with rope lashing, allowing them to be cut so that there is a clear space over which to haul the casualty. Recovery via a boarding ladder makes sense in calm conditions if the MOB is strong enough. If not, a dinghy or life raft can be used as a staging point before recovery. There are various man overboard slings on the market, but some of these have been shown to be dangerously inadequate. If you have one, make sure you've tried it out – there'll be no time to read the instructions with a man in the water.

One technique that has been known to work is to drop the boom into the cockpit and lower the mainsail out of its track on the mast and allow it to fall overboard, creating a giant sling in the water. If the casualty can clamber into this sling the halyard can then be winched up and the recovery raised and rolled on board. That's the theory – but again this technique should be practised if you may end up relying on it to save a life.

QUOTES ON BOATS

Twenty years from now you will be more disappointed by the things that you didn't do than by the ones you did do. So throw off the bowlines. Sail away from the safe harbour. Catch the trade winds in your sails. Explore. Dream. Discover.
Mark Twain, author

SEEING RED

During New Zealand's successful America's Cup challenge in 1995, Kiwi skipper Peter Blake, who was later knighted, wore the same pair of red socks throughout as Team New Zealand went through the campaign winning all but one of their races. The only race they lost was when Blake was rested. Before the final, team sponsors manufactured tens of thousands of pairs of Blake's lucky red socks which sold out in days in New Zealand. They won the final, beating Dennis Connor's American team in a 5-0 drubbing. Blake was killed by pirates during an exploration of the Amazon River in 2001, but red socks are still associated with sailing and success in his homeland.

Length, in metres, of Playstation, the giant catamaran that sailed non-stop around the world in 58 days

SAILING STEREOTYPES

The yacht club bore

What the yacht club bore does not know about sailing is not worth knowing – at least that is what he thinks. This truly awful breed of sailor can be found in every club around the country and will almost always be alone. He will certainly be male, though may bring a wife who will remain silent at all times.

The bore doesn't do much sailing these days, but will have one or two war stories up his sleeve to prove his authority. No longer sailing himself, he is in the perfect position to tell everyone else how to do it. He absorbs all sorts of sailing trivia, which he will regurgitate at any opportunity, completely oblivious to the fact that his audience may not be showing any interest at all. The bore will generally target lone victims, as their chances of a quick getaway without appearing rude are slim. Indeed it is the politeness of other members that allows the bore to carry on. His thick skin prevents him from noticing that his fellow members find him dull while their good manners prevent them from telling him.

WHAT A PRO

Procedural words, or 'prowords', are used in radio communications to increase the brevity and clarity of communications. As you will see, people only say 'Over and out' in the movies.

Say again	To ask for a repetition
I say again	To give a repetition
Correction	Said before correcting part of a message
Spell	Said before using the phonetic alphabet to spell a word
This is	To identify caller
Over	Invitation to reply
Out	The end of the conversation. No reply is expected.

HOW POSH

Once upon a time, long before the advent of discount airlines, if you wanted to journey to a far continent you had to do so by boat. It would take months to sail to India or Australia and comfort was key as the sun beat down on your liner. Air-conditioning was yet to be invented and cabins that faced the afternoon sun could become intolerably hot. The cooler, shaded side of the boat was on the port side as you headed south to the colonies, and on the starboard side as you headed back. Of course a premium had to be paid for such luxury and only the smartest could travel Port Out Starboard Home – or POSH as it became known.

Britain may not be a very big country but her coastline is extremely varied and there is a part of it that will suit every sailor. Locals are immensely proud of their own home waters and will argue fiercely with anyone who claims to know a better spot to keep a boat. This is strange as many of those doing the arguing have never sailed, or perhaps even visited, the area that they are maligning. One can, very crudely, break up the principal sailing areas of the British Isles into broad regions. Here are the arguments for and against them.

West Country

Stretching from The Isles of Scilly, standing sentinel in the Atlantic, to the River Exe in Devon, there is no cruising ground like it in the British Isles – at least that it what the locals will tell you, though many yachtsmen from elsewhere also rate it as their favourite sailing spot. The coast is varied with sandy beaches, tall cliffs and plenty of wooded valleys up which rivers meander, creating perfect anchorages and sheltered harbours. Helford, Falmouth, Fowey, Plymouth, Salcombe, Dartmouth and Exmouth are all delightful and don't have the crowds that are synonymous with the waters around the Solent.

The South

More yachts are kept between Weymouth and Dover than in the rest of the country put together, and the majority of them are squeezed into marinas and on to moorings around the Solent. Fans of these waters will tell you of the convenience of it all, the variety of nearby harbours to visit, and the fact that there's always something going on. Detractors will point out the astronomical prices of marina berths, the crowded waters and the fact that you have to share the sea with huge shipping.

The East Coast

The southeastern corner of Britain is characterised in the minds of many sailors as flat and muddy, and parts of it do live up to this rather drab reputation. However, many of those who sail there would not swap it for anywhere else in the world. The network of rivers and estuaries, sandbanks and mudflats means that one can sail on the East Coast for a lifetime and never be bored. Having a boat that can settle on the mud is essential for fully exploring this potterer's paradise.

Western Scotland

Few yachtsmen make it this far but those who do declare it to be God's own cruising ground. The scenery is majestic with a backdrop of mountains and moorland that sweeps down to the sea. Compared with most other parts of the country you have the sea to yourself and can explore the numerous islands with their sandy beaches and snug anchorages protected from the swell of the open ocean. On the other hand it can be cold and it does rain an awful lot.

Speed, in knots, reached by the world's fastest kite-surfer, Emmanuel Taub

WORDS ON THE WATER

By the Lord, Jack, you may say what you will; but I'll be damned if it was not Davey Jones himself. I know him by his saucer eyes, his three rows of teeth, his horns and tail, and the blue smoke that came out of his nostrils. What does the blackguard hell's baby want with me? I am sure I have never committed murder except in the way of my profession, nor wronged any man whatsoever since I first went to sea.

Tobias Smollett, *Commodore Trunnion*

MEDITERRANEAN WINDS AND WHERE THEY BLOW FROM

Northerly	*Tramontana*
North-easterly	*Greco*
Easterly	*Levante*
South-easterly	*Sirocco*
Southerly	*Ostro*
South-westerly	*Libeccio*
Westerly	*Ponente*
North-westerly	*Maestro*

THE BOTTOM CLEANERS

If you think your car gets grubby after a few weeks on the road, spare a thought for the bottom of your boat. All manner of animal and vegetable life makes its home on yachts' hulls – and the more stuff that's growing there, the slower the boat will go. Antifouling paint helps to slow down the growth but cannot stop it altogether, meaning that a jolly good scrub is required from time to time. If you've got the money, you can ask the boatyard to crane the boat out and blast her down with a high pressure hose. If you're strapped for cash you go round in a dinghy with a deck brush – though you'll probably need to don swimming trunks and a mask to clean the keel.

There is an alternative, however, in the shape of the BoatScrubber. This cunning invention works exactly like a carwash – but for boats. You sail up to a pontoon, moor your yacht and hand over your money. A button is pushed and two large round brushes rise out from the water, detect where the vessel starts, and begin to spin. They work their way down each side of the hull, slowly but surely, and rid it of all the marine life that has been growing there. They can handle almost any sort of keel, but can't do the inner sides of catamarans. Once their work is complete they sink beneath the waves and you sail away with a lovely clean bottom.

The heads

The heads is what sailors call a lavatory on board a boat and there is nowhere else that the harsh, unromantic realities of sailing are more apparent. Imagine the scene: you're at sea and the boat is heeled over. You've been on deck in your full oilskins and boots and now need to visit the heads. Your trousers have built-in braces meaning that you'll need to take your jacket off to get them down. This done, you are faced with a choice. Take off your oilskin trousers in the saloon (this will involve removing your boots too and getting your socks wet), or try to merely lower them to your ankles in the heads. You opt for the latter but find the toilet cubicle is so small, with so little elbow room, that the dexterity of a contortionist is required to achieve your goal. Trousers eventually dropped, you lower yourself towards the bowl, which rises and falls with the pitching boat. The toilet will have been set as low as possible so that your knees will be near your ears when you finally make contact. Now you have to remember to twist numerous stopcocks and flick various switches. Failure to do so will result in water flooding into the bowl and the boat sinking, or worse, the toilet blocking. As you try and remember what to pump and when, the boat lurches and a wave of whatever is in the bowl splashes up against you. You hastily complete your business and man the pump to flush the bowl. But woe of woes! There is a blockage somewhere in the yards of too-thin pipe that snake from the loo to the sea. With a heavy heart you recall the ominous warning during the skipper's briefing: 'You block it, you clear it.'

GALE WARNINGS

In nautical parlance, a gale is a period of severe weather with winds of at least Force Eight (34-40 knots). If such winds (and the gusts reaching 43-51 knots that accompany them) are expected within a weather forecasting sea area, then a gale warning for that area will be issued. Severe gales involve winds of at least Force Nine (41-47 knots) and gusts of up to 60 knots. A storm occurs if winds reach Force 10 (48-55 knots) with gusts of up to 68 knots.

Gales that are described as 'imminent' are expected to arrive within six hours of the warning's time of issue. 'Soon' indicates an arrival within 6-12 hours and 'later' means more than 12 hours from time of issue.

Strong wind warnings are issued when winds of Force Six (22-27 knots) or above are expected up to five miles offshore.

HOW CHILLING

Low temperatures combined with strong winds can create a dangerous cocktail for those at sea. There are officially seven levels of wind chill factor:

I   Comfortable with normal precautions.
II Work becomes uncomfortable on overcast days unless properly clothed.
III Work becomes hazardous. Heavy clothing is necessary.
IV Unprotected skin will freeze with direct exposure over a long period.
V   Unprotected skin will freeze within one minute.
VI Adequate face protection is mandatory. Work alone is prohibited.
VII Survival efforts are required.

QUOTES ON BOATS

Upon acquiring his first boat the yachtsman discovers that its use is going to involve intimate, personal contact with rope and cordage, and to a far greater extent than he ever anticipated.
Hervey Garrett Smith, marine illustrator

ILS AIMENT LA VOILE

The British pride themselves on being a seafaring nation. They hark back to the days of Drake and Nelson and feel all warm inside. They also look back on their more recent pioneers, men like Sir Francis Chichester and Sir Robin Knox-Johnston, who led the way in single-handed offshore racing. Britain certainly has a lot to be proud of, and good reason to love the sea and sailors, but compared to the French we care not a jot.

The top sailors in France are given the sort of adulation and press coverage reserved for the best British football players. The crowds that turn out to wave off the single-handers at the start of a race in France are counted in their hundreds of thousands. Sponsors gladly write cheques for large sums, confident in the knowledge that the coverage they'll receive in the French press will justify the cost.

Why are the French so mad on sailing? No one is sure. It is part of their culture and always has been. French children are encouraged to sail in a way that few British ones are, and those who go on to make it big know that they will be household names. Britain may have won the Battle of Trafalgar, but in many ways the French are winning the war of the sea.

But Jonah rose up to flee unto Tarshish from the presence of the Lord, and went down to Joppa; and he found a ship going to Tarshish: so he paid the fare thereof, and went down into it, to go with them unto Tarshish from the presence of the Lord.

But the Lord sent out a great wind into the sea, and there was a mighty tempest in the sea, so that the ship was like to be broken.

Then the mariners were afraid, and cried every man unto his god, and cast forth the wares that were in the ship into the sea, to lighten it of them. But Jonah was gone down into the sides of the ship; and he lay, and was fast asleep.

So the shipmaster came to him, and said unto him, 'What meanest thou, O sleeper? arise, call upon thy God, if so be that God will think upon us, that we perish not.'

And they said every one to his fellow, 'Come, and let us cast lots, that we may know for whose cause this evil is upon us.' So they cast lots, and the lot fell upon Jonah.

Then said they unto him, 'Tell us, we pray thee, for whose cause this evil is upon us; what is thine occupation? and whence comest thou? what is thy country? and of what people art thou?'

And he said unto them, 'I am an Hebrew; and I fear the Lord, the God of heaven, which hath made the sea and the dry land.'

Then were the men exceedingly afraid, and said unto him, 'Why hast thou done this?' For the men knew that he fled from the presence of the Lord, because he had told them.

Then said they unto him, 'What shall we do unto thee, that the sea may be calm unto us?' for the sea wrought, and was tempestuous.

And he said unto them, 'Take me up, and cast me forth into the sea; so shall the sea be calm unto you: for I know that for my sake this great tempest is upon you.'

Nevertheless the men rowed hard to bring it to the land; but they could not: for the sea wrought, and was tempestuous against them.

Wherefore they cried unto the Lord, and said, 'We beseech thee, O Lord, we beseech thee, let us not perish for this man's life, and lay not upon us innocent blood: for thou, O Lord, hast done as it pleased thee.'

So they took up Jonah, and cast him forth into the sea: and the sea ceased from her raging.

Then the men feared the Lord exceedingly, and offered a sacrifice unto the Lord, and made vows.

Now the Lord had prepared a great fish to swallow up Jonah. And Jonah was in the belly of the fish three days and three nights.

Jonah 1; 3-17

'Yes Miss Jones, it was a very good dive,
but please don't do that again.'

QUOTES ON BOATS

The pessimist complains about the wind; the optimist
expects it to change; the realist adjusts the sails.
William Arthur Ward, scholar and churchman

THE ONLY WAY IS UP

The compass is perhaps the yachtsman's greatest friend, but all is not lost if your trusty compass goes over the side – as long as you're wearing a watch you'll be all right. You will need to know which hemisphere you're in.

Hold the watch flat and point the hour hand at the sun. The line bisecting the angle made between the hour hand and the figure 12 will point approximately south. The reciprocal of this line will be north. In the Southern Hemisphere the bisecting angle points north. If you got rid of your old watch in favour of a flashy digital model you will have to wait until nightfall to work out where you are going. In the Northern Hemisphere the full moon is South at midnight (GMT).

SEEING RED

Red sun at night, sailors delight;
Red sky in the morning, sailors take warning.

On a normal day the sun appears red as it sets and is orange when it pops up the next morning. Changes to these colours tell sailors (and shepherds too) that some sort of weather disturbance is on its way. If the morning sun seems very red, the air it is shining through will be unusually dry, cold air, and it is safe to predict that wind and rain will soon follow.

WHEN IS A KNOT NOT A KNOT?

When it has another name:

Angler's loop
Clinging clara
Duncan loop
Englishman's loop
Eskimo bowline
Fisherman's bend
Granny knot
Highwayman's hitch
Italian hitch
Surgeon's knot
Turk's head
Waggoner's hitch

ROYALTY AT A PRICE

If you fancy going for a sail but want to do so in style and not sacrifice your creature comforts, then why not sign up for a cruise on the $40 million Royal Clipper? She's a five-masted sailing ship – the only one in the world – and unlike on some cruising vessels, the sails actually work. The five tonnes of canvas that she can hoist cover an area of nine tennis courts and drive her through the water at 17 knots. Most of the 42 sails can be hoisted or furled via computer-controlled hydraulic winches, meaning that crew rarely need to climb the rigging. Beneath the sails are 228 cabins boasting all the luxuries of life that one could ask for. Restaurants offer the finest cuisine served in opulent surroundings, giving the passengers the best of both worlds – the romance of sail with the comfort of a cruise liner. And the price for all this luxury? £12,000 per person per week – the price of a second-hand yacht.

A NAUTICAL JOKE

A young woman was so depressed that she decided to end her life by throwing herself into the ocean. She went down to the docks and was about to leap into the freezing water when a handsome young sailor saw her tottering on the edge of the pier and crying.

He took pity on her and said, 'Look, you've got a lot to live for. I'm off to Australia in the morning, and if you like, I can stow you away on my ship. I'll take good care of you and bring you food every day.' Moving closer he slipped his arm round her shoulder and added, 'I'll keep you happy, and you'll keep me happy.'

The girl nodded yes. After all, what did she have to lose? That night, the sailor brought her aboard and hid her in a lifeboat. From then on every night he brought her three sandwiches and a piece of fruit, and they made passionate love until dawn. Three weeks later, during a routine inspection, she was discovered by the captain.

'What are you doing here?' the Captain asked.

'I have an arrangement with one of the sailors,' she explained. 'I get food and a trip to Australia, and he's screwing me.'

'He sure is,' the Captain said, 'this is the Isle of Wight ferry.'

HOW TO READ A BAROMETER

Every yacht should have a barometer on board. The rule of thumb is that the higher the pressure the more settled the weather, and vice versa.

Falling steadily	A sign of bad weather
Rising steadily	A sign of good weather
Falling rapidly	Bad weather and gales coming soon
Rising rapidly	Better weather, though it may be short-lived

WHAT COLOUR ARE YOUR WELLIES?

There are some rules about what colour wellies should be worn where, and all sailors would do well to observe them. People who work in the country wear black wellington boots. Those who live there – or would like to – wear green wellies. Blue wellies are reserved for use at sea and in no circumstances should be worn more than a mile inland. Red wellies are worn only by children jumping in puddles and Frenchmen. Yellow wellies have been worn at sea, but not in the last 30 years. Despite the fact that a good quality rubber boot was adequate for generation after generation of sailor, the modern yottie is starting to shun rubber in favour of various breathable materials. Mixtures of GoreTex (blue) and leather (brown) are popular, but expect to pay £200 or more to keep your feet dry.

NAUTICAL PUZZLES

1. Pick a number between one and 10 (including one or 10).
2. Multiply your number by nine.
3. Add together the two digits that make up the number created in step two.
4. Subtract five from the number created in step three.
5. Find the letter in the alphabet that corresponds to the number created in step four, ie: 1=A, 2=B, 3=C, etc.
6. Pick a country in Europe that starts with the letter you found in step five.
7. Pick a part of a yacht that starts with the last letter of your country.
8. Pick a colour that starts with the last letter of your yacht part.

Turn to page 153 to find out what sort of boat you sail

SWALLOWS AND AMAZONS FOR EVER!

Arthur Ransome's Swallows and Amazons stories, first published in the 1930s, introduced many young children to sailing. The main characters were two groups of children who go sailing, camping and exploring in the Lake District.

Swallows: John • Susan • Titty • Roger • Bridget

Amazons: Nancy • Peggy

SAILING TERMS THAT CONFUSE LANDLUBBERS

Boom

Not what a cannon does, nor half of Basil Brush's laugh, the boom is the pole that extends horizontally from the bottom of the mast. The boom is positioned on most yachts at such a height that it will take the top of your head off in the same manner as one may remove the top of an egg. The most effective way to carry out such a marine lobotomy is by gybing, allowing the back of the boat to pass through the wind. This causes the boom, which holds the outside corner (or clew) of the mainsail, to swing through about 180 degrees in a split second, accelerating all the time. Gybes can be carried out in a controlled manner with the helmsman calling out a warning, then calling out 'Gybe-o' just before the boom swings across. Accidental gybes are more commonly accompanied by a curse, with the helmsman calling out 'Gybe-o' just after the boom has whistled millimetres past your ear.

QUOTES ON BOATS

Whether the weather be fine, or whether the weather be not;
We'll weather the weather, whatever the weather;
Whether we like it or not.
Anon

WHAT ALL SAILORS SHOULD KNOW

If you spend enough time afloat you will learn all these things the hard way.

Always put on your oilskin jacket as soon as you think about it.
The same thing is said about reefing a sail, but the jacket idea is much more important. Yachtsmen constantly ignore this piece of advice and consequently don their jacket only after a stray wave has sploshed against the hull and down their neck.

Obey the rules about the heads
A ship's toilet can be a temperamental thing and if the skipper tells you to rotate three times and say a prayer before you use it, then do so. Likewise, the rule that you should pump 30 times when flushing means exactly that. You might think that everyone on board is going over the top with the whole flushing thing, but that may be because you have never spent a long time on a boat with a smelly loo or had to take one apart to clear a blockage.

Work out where the wind is coming from
There are lots of ways to do this. The wind and waves generally come from the same direction, as do the clouds. There's likely to be a wind indicator atop the mast and even a display on the instrument panel in the cockpit. You can even lick a finger, hold it up and see which side feels cooler. If in doubt, you can always ask. This is important because only when you are sure you know where the wind is coming from can you then throw the dregs of your tea (or have a pee) in the opposite direction with confidence.

Stow everything
Those on land talk of storage, those on boats speak of stowage. The concepts are identical except for one important factor: stowage is storage at 30 degrees of heel. If you put something in a cupboard or a drawer at home, you can be confident that it will be there when you come to retrieve it. The same cannot be said for an object at sea unless it has been stowed in a seaworthy fashion. This means that whenever you put something down you have to imagine the boat as though she were bashing to windward, heeled over on her side. Such violent movements turn shelves into ski jumps and cupboards into catapults. In such conditions storage will just not do – only stowage will suffice.

As the day wore on the weather became worse and so we hove-to upon port tack. We were then somewhere about the middle of the Gulf Stream. During the night the wind eased, but in the morning the sky began to clear and the wind shifted to the north-west. Soon it was blowing a whole gale. The Gulf Stream in a gale of wind must surely be one of the finest sights in the world. In northern waters there is nothing which can be compared with it, and though the seas may perhaps run as big, they are not so steep and, by comparison, sea and sky are almost colourless. Here, there was a blazing sun, a huge sea (for some hours the average height from trough to crest was about 46 to 50 feet by careful measurement) which was so steep that the breaking crests were out of all proportion to those upon ordinary steep-sea waves and the colours were extraordinarily vivid. The Gulf Stream water is of the darkest sapphire blue, which seems to have no trace of green in it, such as there is in the other parts of the Atlantic. As one approaches the northern limit of the Stream curious patches of brownish-green water appear in the blue, and when one has actually left the Stream and is sailing in the waters which flow south from the Arctic this brownish-green colour is very noticeable.

EG Martin,
Deep-water Cruising

THE COASTAL NAVIGATOR'S BASIC KIT

Binoculars • Chart • Course-plotter
Dividers (drawing compasses)
Electronic log • GPS set
Handbearing compass
Pencils • Rubber • Ruler
Steering compass • Stopwatch

CRUISING COCKTAILS

Salty Dog

A simple cocktail using ingredients that one may actually have on board. Take a glass and moisten the rim (saliva works well) then invert onto a saucer of salt. Add one measure of gin and top up with grapefruit juice. If time is short you can dispense with the salt as most things on board are already encrusted in it. Vodka can be used as a substitute for gin, as can rum, whisky and most fuel additives. If required, replace grapefruit juice with orange juice, apple juice, water or more gin.

Why, in reality, sail always gives way to power.

THE MINI-TRANSAT

Open 60 yachts are the Formula One of the sailing world. These monster machines are sailed by lone skippers across the world's oceans at staggering speeds. They're big, they're fast and they're very expensive. Finding sponsorship to build or buy an Open 60 is as much a challenge as sailing one, and companies want to know that they are giving their money to a sailor who will win races. To prove their worth and learn the ropes, aspiring yachtsmen compete in the Mini-Transat.

This race, from France to the Caribbean, is for the most promising solo sailors who want to make it big. They compete in the Open 6.5 class – high performance 'pocket rockets' that demand nerves of steel as their skippers push them to the limit to cross the 4,800 miles of the storm-swept Atlantic.

The boats may be no more than 6.5m (21ft) long and the materials of which they can be built are limited, but beyond these stipulations there are few design restrictions. This freedom makes the class a breeding ground for new ideas and cutting-edge technology that often go on to appear in more conservative racing and cruising yachts. Twin rudders, canting keels and water ballast were all proven among the Mini-Transat fleet.

THEY SHOULD HAVE CALLED HIM TIN-TIN

An inventory of the many tins carried by Chay Blyth on his record-breaking solo circumnavigation of the world against prevailing winds and currents in1970.

Irish stew	2 doz	Chicken soup	1 doz
Steak and kidney	2 doz	Treacle sponge puddings	2 doz
Lamb and veg	2 doz	Custard	2 doz
Beef and veg	2 doz	Plums	1 doz
Spaghetti bolognese	1 doz	Celery	2 doz
Sweetcorn	1 doz	Mushroom soup	2 doz
Peas	2 doz	Blackcurrants	1 doz
Carrots	2 doz	Pear	1 doz
Celery soup	2 doz	Mandarin oranges	1 doz
Tomatoes	2 doz	Peaches	1 doz
Potatoes	2 doz	Strawberries	1 doz
Mixed Veg	2 doz	Condensed milk	2 doz
Steak and kidney pudding	2 doz	Evaporated milk	2 doz
Corned beef	2 doz	Nestlé cream	2 doz
Hams	6	Sardines	2 doz
Beef casserole	1 doz	Royal game soup	1 doz
Scotch broth	1 doz	Prawns	1 doz
Vegetable salad	1 doz	Salmon	1 doz
Potato salad	1 doz	Tuna	1 doz
Tongues	2 doz	Wall's pork sausages	1 doz
Braised mutton	1 doz	Butter	7
Steak and kidney pies	2 doz	Luncheon meat	6
Steak pasties	2 doz	Mushrooms	9
Lamb garni and veg	1 doz	Kippers	2 doz
Braised steak	2 doz	Haggis	1 doz
Beans and minced beef	1 doz	Tomato ketchup	1 doz
Macaroni	1 doz	Sandwich spread	1 doz
Raspberries	1 doz	Ideal sauce	1 doz
Fruit salad	1 doz		
Sultana	1 doz	*Washed down with...*	
Golden honey	1 doz	Long-life milk	150 pints
Sponge puddings	1 doz	Whisky	6 bottles
Savoury minced steak	2 doz	Gin	6 bottles
Beans and pork sausage	1 doz	Drambuie	6 bottles
Oxtail soup	1 doz	Guinness	20 doz

QUOTES ON BOATS

The best noise in all the world is the rattle of the anchor chain when one comes into harbour at last and lets it go over the bows.
Hilaire Belloc, author

THE BEAUTY OF S&S

Sparkman and Stephens are synonymous with excellence in yacht design. S&S, as the partnership is better known, came about when the Stephens brothers, Olin and Rod, joined forces with Drake Sparkman in the late 1920s. The dominance of their designs has been unparalleled, from 6-, 8- and 12-metre boats to America's Cup yachts. Cruising yachts from the drawing board of Sparkman and Stephens are almost guaranteed to be fast, stable, safe and strong. The team produced many racing yachts which are acknowledged classics – a number of which are still being raced. Photographs of beautiful S&S yachts such as Dorade, Vim, Nyala, Columbia, Stormy Weather, Intrepid and Courageous fill many a stunning coffee table book, yet pride and trust in your vessel are not restricted to these craft – they come as standard with any Sparkman and Stephens design.

NAUTICAL PUZZLES

You are sailing down the Atlantic from Britain to South America. You do not have any means of electronic navigation, and the sky is constantly obscured by clouds so that the sun, moon and stars are never visible. How do you know when you have crossed the equator?

Answer on page 153

SAILING TERMS THAT CONFUSE LANDLUBBERS

Log

Another of those words that means several things at sea, including a large chunk of wood, as in 'Oh dear we've just hit a log.' Precisely speaking, a ship's log is the device that records the distance a vessel has travelled. Such distances are recorded in a logbook, commonly shortened to log. This is the sort of log made famous by the captain of the Starship Enterprise. The ship's log contains all the details of where you have been, where you are now and where you are going. As well as positions, courses and speeds, the responsible skipper will note down the weather forecast and any other relevant information. Some logbooks are works of science, others are works of fiction that have been filled in after arrival for the sake of appearances, while yet others are works of art, complete with sketches of the local flora and fauna. The use of the word originates from the floating, wooden sort of log that was thrown overboard with a knotted line attached and used to calculate a vessel's speed.

GO TO SEA ON A 'C'

A surprising number of types of boat begin with the letter 'C'

Cableship	vessel fitted for laying underwater cable
Caique	small traditional Turkish or Greek sailing boat
Camship	merchant ship armed with catapult to launch a plane
Canoa	sloop-rigged fishing boat from Brazil
Canoe	narrow open boat, powered by paddles or sails
Capital ship	the most important warship in a navy's fleet
Caracore	fast Indonesian sailing vessel
Caravel	small Mediterranean trading vessel
Cargo ship	any vessel that carries freight rather than passengers
Carrack	large European trading vessel with high fore and aft castles
Cartel	ship used in times of war to negotiate between enemies
Casco	small, flat-bottomed cargo boat from the Philippines
Catamaran	any twin-hulled vessel
Cat boat	beamy, shallow sailing boat from Cape Cod in the USA
Chasse-Marée	lugger used by French customs and pirates
Clipper	very fast sailing ships of the nineteenth century
Coaster	any vessel employed in coastal trade
Coble	flat-bottomed fishing boat from north-east England
Cock boat	any boat carried on board another
Cog	merchant ship of the fifteenth century
Coracle	small boat made from stretching skins over a wicker frame
Corbita	merchant ship of Imperial Rope
Corvette	flush-decked warship of the eighteenth century
Cromster	two-masted Elizabethan vessel
Cunner	dug-out canoe with two sails
Cutter	yacht with a mainsail and two foresails

NINE WAYS TO SAY HULL

English	*hull*
French	*coque*
German	*Rumpf*
Dutch	*romp*
Danish	*skrog*
Spanish	*casco*
Italian	*carena*
Portuguese	*casco*
Turkish	*karina*

54 *Year in the nineteenth century that the oldest continually operating tidal gauge in the Western Hemisphere was built in San Francisco*

SLOW DOWN!

Speed is generally regarded as a good thing for any yachtsman. Whether racing around the buoys or cruising from one port to another, most sailors will try and have their boats sailing as quickly as possible. There are, however, rare instances when too much speed can be a bad thing.

If a yachtsman is caught out by rough weather and finds himself at sea with huge waves and high winds, then thoughts turn from speed to survival. Sailing into the wind is likely to result in damage to the boat; running before the wind – in the same direction as the winds and waves – reduces the pressures on yacht and crew but carries its own dangers. Yachts will be lifted up by the waves and start surfing down their fronts, gathering speed. The faster the boat goes, the greater the risk that she will not be able to steer a straight course and will be pushed sideways with a wave powering down on top of her and possibly rolling her over.

Reducing the vessel's speed is the key to survival in such a situation. In such extreme circumstances sails will already have been lowered, the wind blowing on the yacht's mast and hull being enough to drive her through the water.

A variety of objects can be towed in the water to act as a brake and are known as drogues. Extremely long lengths of rope can be towed, each end secured to the stern and the loop being dragged behind. Small sails can also be towed and many experts recommend towing a car tyre or two. Purpose-made drogues look like parachutes made of straps of canvas.

THE SYDNEY-HOBART RACE

The race from Sydney to Hobart in Tasmania is as important a fixture in the Australian racing calendar as the Fastnet Race is to British yachtsmen. The 630-mile event was first held in 1945 and soon became a classic with an international field. It takes place on Boxing Day and attracts some of the best yachtsmen in the world. And just as the Fastnet will always be associated with the event of 1979 when 15 lives were lost, so will the Sydney-Hobart be forever associated with the events of 1998.

The fleet of 115 boats was hit by a severe storm as it crossed the Bass Strait between the Australian mainland and Tasmania. An area of massive high pressure, known as a 'bomb', had formed and winds of 78mph were reported, kicking up seas as high as 10m (33ft).

A total of 55 yachtsmen had to be rescued. Seven yachts were abandoned, five of which subsequently sank. Only 44 boats reached the finish line and six yachtsmen never made it back to dry land.

SEA SAYINGS

First rate

From the sixteenth century until steam-powered ships took over, British naval ships were rated as to the number of heavy cannon they carried. A ship of 100 or more guns was a First Rate line-of-battle ship. Second Rates carried 90 to 98 guns; Third Rates 64 to 89 guns; Fourth Rates 50 to 60 guns. Frigates carrying 20 to 48 guns were Fifth- and Sixth-rated.

THREE SHEETS TO THE WIND

Classic pub names with a nautical theme

The Albion • The Bell • The Blue Anchor

Bramley Moore • The Britannia • The British Pilot

The Chase • Diver's Arms • Hope Inn

The Kelly • Look Out • Lord Nelson

Man o'War • The Marine • The Monarch

Neptune Inn • The New Ferry Tavern

Old Endeavour • Royal Oak • The Ship

The Stack • The Telegraph • The Trafalgar

The Victory • The Vigilant • The Western

WORDS ON THE WATER

One night came on a hurricane,
The sea was mountains rolling,
When Barney Buntline turned his quid,
And said to Billy Bowling:
'A strong nor-wester's blowing, Bill;
Hark! don't ye hear it roar, now?
Lord help 'em, how I pities them
Unhappy folks on shore now!

'Foolhardy chaps who live in towns,
What danger they are all in,
And now lie quaking in their beds,
For fear the roof should fall in;
Poor creatures! how they envies us,
And wishes, I've a notion,
For our good luck, in such a storm,
To be upon the ocean!'

Charles Dibdin, _The Sailor's Consolation_

CROSSING THE LINE

Crossing the equator is an unforgettable moment for any yachtsman. Not only does it mark their passing from one hemisphere to another, it also is likely to involve their being smeared with all manner of foul-smelling nasties before receiving a bucket of water over the head.

Such humiliating rituals stretch back into the mists of nautical history but are still keenly followed today, especially if there is someone on board who still remembers their own initiation. The style of ceremony varies from vessel to vessel but should involve someone dressed up as King Neptune who presides over proceedings and before whom the equator virgins are paraded. Neptune gives his orders, the gunk is administered and everyone has a drink and a laugh. If only all royal courts were such fun.

NOR ANY A DROP TO DRINK

If disaster befalls you in home waters, the odds are that you won't have to wait too long before being rescued. Things are different if you're in the middle of the ocean. In such a scenario, water must be your first concern. If you have enough water you will probably live. Without it you will certainly die. If you are stuck at sea for long enough your reserves of water will eventually run out. Many ocean-going yachtsmen now carry water makers on board that can extract drinking water from the sea. However they can be very inefficient and are not always reliable – but don't despair. Look to the heavens instead because that's where salvation lies in the form of rainwater. If you wait long enough the skies will open and you'll need to be ready to make the most of it. Various techniques can be employed to catch rainwater and you don't need disaster to strike before you try them out. Water that hits sails can be chan-nelled to run off one area and simple canvas rain-catchers can be made to trap this water and lead it to a storage container. Special catchers can also be stretched out between the winches in the cockpit and the collected water led via a pipe to the cabin – allowing water to be caught without the crew getting drenched.

The simplest method of all is to allow the first few moments of rain to wash the decks of salt and debris and then to remove the cap to the yacht's water tank. This is usually positioned on the edge of the side deck, meaning that water running aft will flow straight into the tank. It may be necessary to direct the flow to make sure as much water as possible ends up in the tank.

By using techniques such as these many sailors have survived certain death through dehydration while others have been able to voyage to lands that would otherwise have been beyond their reach.

Given the choice between going to sea with an expert sailor or with a good skipper, most people would pick the good skipper every time. The expert may be able to get the boat sailing faster, may be able to plot its position to the nearest inch and tie a bowline with his teeth, but if he's not a good skipper too, it'll all be for nought.

Technical expertise can be learnt, but the people skills required of a good skipper are altogether more subtle. Boats can be stressful places with wind howling through the rigging, waves breaking onto the deck, and the whole thing shifting up and down. A good skipper realises that what is required is calm, not additional stress. His commands are authoritative but polite. He instills confidence instead of making his crew wonder what all the fuss is about. Above all

this, the super skipper does not assume knowledge. 'Pull the red rope! The red one!' screams the expert sailor at his novice crew. 'I can't see a red one!' wails the crew. Our expert has forgotten that the 'red rope' is actually white with a red thread running through it.

Things happen slowly on a good skipper's boat. There's plenty of warning before anything is done and everyone is told what will happen and what he or she must do. The expert will be barking instructions as the boom swings across and the sails start to flap. The good skipper pours oil on troubled waters, the expert pours water on boiling oil.

But above and beyond all these niceties is the fact that the good skipper ensures that the kettle is always on and the tea keeps coming. That's the real secret to a happy ship.

RECOMMENDED ANCHOR WEIGHTS

Anchor type	Yacht length (feet)	Recommended weight (kilos)
Bruce	32	5
	46	10
CQR	30-40	9-11
	40-50	11-16
Delta	30-40	10
	40-50	16
Danforth	36	7.3
	45	19
Spade	34	15
	51	20

WORDS ON THE WATER

In an anchorage where there is no tidal stream, all normal yachts lie head to wind, though they will sheer about from side to side as puffs of wind catch them on one bow or the other. Those with chain cables will lie more steadily than those with rope cables, partly because of the friction created when the yacht on sheering tries to drag a bight of chain over the seabed, and partly because she will have only half the scope that the yacht lying to rope will have out. Therefore, when Susan and I come into a crowded anchorage, we look round to see which yachts are lying to rope and which to chain; avoiding the former, we let go near the latter with the comforting knowledge that we and our neighbours will all behave much alike. Conversely, it is sensible for the man who uses rope to choose an anchorage near other rope users, and not foul up with his wild gyrations the area where the diehard chain-users are lying steadily. Both they and we avoid if we possibly can anchoring anywhere near multihulls, for they with their great windage and slight grip on the water do sometimes behave in the oddest manner.

Eric Hiscock, *Come Aboard*

TRADITIONAL NAUTICAL MEASUREMENTS

1 fathom = six feet or two yards
1 cable = 608 feet, 200 yards or 100 fathoms
1 sea or nautical mile = 6,080 feet or 10 cables or 2,000 yards
1 knot = one sea mile per hour
1 knot = 1.1515 miles per hour

SAILING TERMS THAT CONFUSE LANDLUBBERS

Sheet

Crisp white sheets are never found on board boats, though salty and slightly damp ones may be. Real sailors eschew such fanciness and lie on the floor (or sole) in their oilskins in a sleeping bag. There is an altogether more important sort of sheet to be found on board a sailing boat – and it's not a sheet at all. It's a rope. To be more exact, it is the rope that pulls in – or lets out – a sail and will be tweaked almost constantly by the perfectionist yachtsman. To 'sheet in' is to pull in the sheet, and it is common practice to use the name of the sail to which the rope is tied as a prefix. Pulling in the mainsheet thus draws the mainsail towards the centre of the boat. Beware of shouting 'Sheet!' too loudly in French ports.

A CLASSIC MG

Mention the letters 'MG' to a motoring enthusiast and they will conjure up that quintessentially British sports car that allowed a generation of motorists to have a taste of the fast life and own a classic design. For the yachtsman, MG means something different – though the sentiment is very similar. MG, or Maurice Griffiths, was the editor of *Yachting Monthly* for many years as well as being a renowned yacht designer. MG's designs did not aspire to high performance, but they were incredibly popular nonetheless. The Eventide and Waterwitch designs helped make his name, but the Golden Hind is perhaps his most interesting one.

Named after Sir Francis Drake's vessel, the Golden Hind was built by a West Country firm named Hartwells. The company had skilled joiners but little experience of boats, as their principal line of work was the manufacture of coffins. Nevertheless, Hartwells built more than 100 Golden Hinds, which were snapped up by the yachting public looking for a safe, spacious family cruiser that could handle the rough stuff yet still be dried out on her three keels up one of MG's beloved East Coast rivers. In fact the Golden Hind was such a well-loved all-rounder that one yachting journalist declared her 'the Morris Minor of the yachting world'.

NAUTICAL PUZZLES

Which of the following is not a type of double-ended dugout?
Kaep • Popo
Pungy • Tsukpin
Wa Lap
Answer on page 153

LAT OR LONG?

Distance at sea is another of those things that is more complicated than it first appears. A mile is a mile on land, but at sea it is defined as the length of one minute of latitude. As a result the length of a nautical mile varies from 6,108 feet at the Poles to 6,048 feet at the Equator. A standardised International nautical mile is 6,076 feet, or 1,852 metres.

While latitude changes slightly between the Equator and the Poles, longitude changes much more. One minute of longitude is roughly equal to one minute of latitude at the Equator, and at the Poles it is zero. If you think of the lines of longitude meeting at the top and bottom of a globe, you will soon understand why this is so. The longitude scale on a chart must therefore never be used to measure distance.

SEA SAYINGS

Hunky dory

If everything is hunky dory you know there is nothing to worry about – although you might not realise exactly what you're saying. Sailors were certainly carefree when they visited Hunky-Dori, a street in Yokohama, Japan. Hunky-Dori was at the heart of the city's red light district and where every seaman's pleasure was catered for.

NOT IN MY SEA, YOU DON'T

It is generally accepted that a coastal state may exercise sovereignty over a belt of water adjacent to its coast. Most countries agree that this Territorial Sea cannot extend more than 12 miles from the coast. The Territorial Sea of the United Kingdom varies in width from three miles to the full 12 miles.

The Geneva Convention and United Nations Convention* allow vessels to pass through territorial waters if on innocent passage. This means they must not:

- Threaten or use force
- Exercise or practice with weapons
- Collect information (ie, spy)
- Take part in propaganda against the state
- Launch or land aircraft
- Load or unload people or commodities contrary to the laws of the coastal state
- Wilfully pollute
- Fish
- Carry out research or surveying activities
- Carry out any other activity not having direct bearing on the vessel's passage

Not all maritime countries are parties to these conventions

BENEATH THE WAVES

With their lack of gills and fins, men have generally preferred travelling on top of the water rather than beneath it. However, there are records to suggest that simple submarines were thought of as early as 1578. It is unlikely that such vessels were ever constructed, but less than 50 years later a Dutchman named Cornelius Drebbel is believed to have built a watertight vessel with the minimum of positive buoyancy. The boat was driven by 12 oars which emerged through sealed holes and the oarsmen could drive the craft beneath the waves by changing the angle of the oars' blades.

*Charles tried to block his ears to Sarah's complaints.
Rowing across the Atlantic was certainly not the
dream honeymoon he had imagined.*

QUOTES ON BOATS

To deal with men is as fine an art as it is to deal with ships.
Joseph Conrad, novelist

OIL ON TROUBLED WATERS

The thought of filling a canvas bag with fish oil on the deck of a storm-tossed ship may be one that does not appeal, yet this stinking bag may be the key to your survival. Breaking seas pose the greatest risk to a boat in a storm and a layer of oil over the surface of the water helps prevent these dangerous waves – hence the phrase 'pour oil on troubled waters'. Here's how you do it: take a heavy canvas bag about 30cm by 60cm with a narrow neck that can be secured by a tie cord. Jab the bag all over with a thick sail needle or meat skewer. Secure the bag to a rope, fill it with oil and lower it over the wind-ward side. If you don't have a canvas bag and a supply of fish oil to hand, you can pierce a metal oil-can with a small screwdriver, attach a line to the handle and throw that over the side instead. Position the bag or can so that the oil slick forms to windward.

THAT'S DEEP MAN

The deepest waters in the world are to be found above the Mariana Trench in the Pacific Ocean. At 11,000 metres, or about seven miles, the odds of recovering a winch handle that slips over the side are slim.

The deepest point in the Atlantic Ocean is the Puerto Rico Trench at 8,648 metres (28,374 feet) while the deepest point of the Indian Ocean is the Java Trench, some 7,125 metres (23,376 feet) beneath the surface.

LITTLE BOATS THAT CROSSED THE ATLANTIC

Year	Boat name	Length	Skipper	Time
1964	Sjo Ag	12ft	John Riding	67 days
1966	Nonoalca	12ft	Bill Verity	66 days
1968	April Fool	5ft 11⁷⁄₈in	Hugo Vilhen	84 days
1979	Yankee Girl	10ft	Gerry Spiess	54 days
1981	Soddim*	9ft	Christian Marty	37 days
1982	Giltspur	9ft 9in	Tom McClean	50 days
1982	Windswill	9ft	Bill Dunlop	76 days
1982	Toniky-Nou	5ft 10in	Eric Peters	46 days

a windsurfer

SAILING STEREOTYPES

The new boat owner

Money seems to have come easily to the new boat owner. The value of his house, his shares and his company have all gone up and now he needs to spend some of his cash. He's always fancied sailing and pottered about in a dinghy once when he was six. The new boat owner isn't interested in working his way up five feet at a time until he gets a 40-footer in a decade or so. No, he wants a big white yacht and he wants one now. He goes to a boat show and the salesman in the blazer with a big smile assures him that modern boats are so easy to handle these days that the Sunblast 42 is quite suitable for a novice. He writes a cheque and picks up his boat a month later. And it's true – with furling headsail and mainsail, single line reefing and a nice big engine, it does seem that this sailing lark is child's play. So off he pops, the wrong side of the channel buoy and through a fleet of Optimist dinghies. He hasn't got any flares or lifejackets on board as they were extras, and the anchor is still in its box down below. It's at this point that the engine dies, the tide starts to run hard and the fog rolls in and he starts to wish he'd done a course or two before setting sail in his gleaming new boat.

But the worst was not come yet; the storm continued with such fury that the seamen themselves acknowledged they had never seen a worse. We had a good ship, but she was deep laden, and wallowed in the sea, so that the seamen every now and then cried out she would founder. It was my advantage in one respect, that I did not know what they meant by 'founder' till I inquired. However, the storm was so violent that I saw, what is not often seen, the master, the boatswain, and some others more sensible than the rest, at their prayers, and expecting every moment when the ship would go to the bottom.

Daniel Defoe, *Robinson Crusoe*

FLARES ARE BACK IN

The following flares must be carried onboard to comply with Royal Ocean Racing Club rules

Four red parachute
Two orange floating
Four red pinpoint
Four white collision

MIXED MESSAGES

The following conversation is alleged to have taken place between two radio operators – one American, one Canadian.

Canadian: Please divert your course 15 degrees to the south to avoid a collision.

American: Recommend you divert your course 15 degrees to the north to avoid a collision.

Canadian: Negative. You will have to divert your course 15 degrees to the south to avoid a collision.

American: This is the captain of a US navy ship. I say again, divert your course.

Canadian: No. I say again, you divert your course.

American: This is the aircraft carrier USS Lincoln, the second largest ship in the United States Atlantic fleet. We are accompanied by three destroyers, three cruisers and numerous support vessels. I demand that you change your course 15 degrees north – I say again, that's one-five degrees north – or counter-measures will be under-taken to ensure the safety of this ship.

Canadian: This is a lighthouse. Your call.

QUOTES ON BOATS

*The point of a towed tender is that it can be,
and should be, a really good boat and work of art.*
Philip C Bolger, naval architect

IVAN THE TERRIBLE

The Caribbean is a yachtsman's playground. Warm seas, fresh winds, stunning anchorages, beautiful beaches and colourful local culture – it's got it all. It's no wonder that so many yachts gravitate to this sun-kissed corner of the world and often linger there longer than they intended. The Caribbean does have one drawback, however, and that is its location within the hurricane belt. Every year these meteorological menaces sweep northwards, leaving a trail of destruction in their wake. The path of each hurricane is meticulously recorded and thankfully some Caribbean islands are considered to be beyond their reach – or at least they were.

Grenada was one such island thought to be safe from hurricanes, and for this reason hundreds and hundreds of yachts would sail there from all over the Caribbean. Insurers often insisted that yachts passed the hurricane season below the 12 degree line of latitude that passes through the island, and the southerly boatyards would be full every year. Not any more. In the autumn of 2004, Hurricane Ivan swept over Grenada reaping a whirlwind of chaos. Yachts that were sturdily supported were toppled like dominoes – hardly any were left standing as winds of 150mph battered the island. Millions of pounds' worth of damage was caused to yachts that were often the only home of cruising couples who had 'sold up and sailed away' to follow their dream.

The impact on the island and its population was terrible, with homes destroyed and looters running riot in the streets. Thirty-nine people were killed and more than 90% of homes were destroyed. As the winds finally died down, scores of boat-owners emerged to see whether their vessels were where they had left them. Few were. Incredible stories emerged of crews swimming ashore with ropes to secure their boats, and then being trapped in mangrove swamps as the air became thick with flying debris. One skipper stayed on board and could not believe his luck as his yacht was dragged out to sea and then blown safely back to shore after the eye of the storm passed.

The sailors' lack of preparation for Hurricane Ivan was understandable. They had been told that they would be safe beneath the magic 12 degree North line. Indeed, it had been 49 years since a storm of such strength had hit Grenada. Now no one will say when the next one will come.

MASTER AND COMMANDER

The Aubrey-Maturin novels of Patrick O'Brien capture the essence of life at sea at the time of Napoleonic Wars and sell in their millions. In chronological order they are:

Master and Commander • *Post Captain*
HMS Surprise • *The Mauritius Command*
Desolation Island • *The Fortune of War*
The Surgeon's Mate • *The Ionian Mission*
Treason's Harbour • *The Far Side of the World*
The Reverse of the Medal • *The Letter of Marque*
The Thirteen-Gun Salute • *The Nutmeg of Consolation*
The Truelove • *The Wine-Dark Sea*
The Commodore • *The Yellow Admiral*
The Hundred Days • *Blue at the Mizzen*

CATAMARAN

The word 'catamaran' comes from two Tamil words: 'katta', meaning to bind or tie, and 'maram', meaning wood. A catamaran is now commonly thought to be a vessel with two hulls, whether it is a cross-channel ferry, a beach cat like the popular Hobie 16, or a world-girdling, record-breaking, racing machine such as Steve Fossett's Playstation.

The very first catamarans are thought to have been rafts of three or more logs tied together by natives of Sri Lanka. Strangely, the word was also used to refer to a British invention that was briefly popular at the start of the nineteenth century: a lead-lined box that contained explosives and a timing mechanism to create a sort of mine, which was used against the French with limited success. The term 'catamaran' was also given to small rectangular craft that acted as a buffer between a large vessel and a harbour wall. None of these cats should be confused with Cat Boats, which are single-hulled craft used for fishing in the shallow waters around Cape Cod.

RANKS OF ENLISTED SAILORS IN THE ROYAL NAVY

Warrant Officer
Chief Petty Officer
Petty Officer
Leading Seaman
Able Seaman
Ordinary Seaman

Percentage of boaters who say that owning a boat has contributed to their well-being

Running aground is as much a part of sailing as stubbing your toes and getting sunburnt. There are lots of ways to do it, but the preferred medium on which to ground is sand or mud – rock tends to be rather unforgiving.

Once aground you will want to refloat your vessel as quickly as possible. If the tide is rising you can just sit and wait to float off, but if it is ebbing you will need to crack on. Driving the boat backwards using the sails or engine is the first technique to try. If this doesn't work you'll need to reduce the draught of the boat by heeling her over. Harden the sails in and ask the crew to stand amidships on one side. Still no joy? Then lash some heavy objects (sail bags, jerry cans, in-laws) to the end of the boom and push it right out. In an extreme situation you can take a line from the top of the mast to the dinghy which then should be rowed or motored at right angles to the lie of the yacht. This is unlikely to work but helps to pass the time.

Rocking the boat from side to side may dig out a hole around the keel and allow you to slip away. This will take coordina-tion among the crew who must rush from port to starboard and back again.

If you're stuck fast and the tide is ebbing away, then it may be time to think about survival. A rocky bottom could be fatal to your yacht's sides and you should con-sider rigging the boom and spin-naker pole as legs to keep her upright. If you'll be drying right out on a sandy bottom, things are slightly less serious. Row out the anchor so that you won't float away when the tide comes in, then load the dinghy with heavy gear to lighten your craft. Inspect the ground for nasty rocks and shopping trolleys, and use bunk mattresses and sail bags to cush-ion the blow as your pride and joy settles on her sides.

If all else fails and you find your boat on her beam ends and your-self at your wits' end, then don't despair. Simply hang a few fend-ers over the stern to hide your yacht's name, hoist a French ensign and pretend you're a stranger in strange waters. Alter-natively you can don your wellies, hop over the side and start scrub-bing the hull as though that was your intention all along.

QUOTES ON BOATS

To know the laws that govern the winds, and to know that you know them, will give you an easy mind on your voyage around the world; otherwise you may tremble at the appearance of every cloud.
Joshua Slocum, US sailor and first man to
sail around the world single-handed

CRUISING COCKTAILS

Pink Gin

There was a time when gin and Angostura bitters were essential items on board any yacht – especially if the skipper owned a blue blazer and a peaked cap. Those days are melting away like the ice that you may or may not place in your pink gin. Indeed, debate now rages about what exactly should go into this classic: some say water, some say tonic, some say nothing at all. There is one dark corner of the World Wide Web that substitutes grenadine for Angostura bitters – heaven forbid.

A proper cruising yachtsman's Pink Gin should be served thus:

1. Take a cracked plastic tumbler and wipe the rim with your shirt.
2. Add a good measure of gin. The amount will depend on whether the wake of a passing ferry jogs your arm at the vital moment – one can but hope.
3. Take what you hope is a bottle of Angostura Bitters (the label has peeled off and there is a chance that it could be Tabasco or Lea & Perrins) and add a couple of splashes.

Serve without ice (real boats don't have freezers) the moment the mainsail cover has been put on.

NAUTICAL PUZZLES

Rearrange this household object to discover a nautical calamity:
Verandah broom
Answer on page 153

WORDS ON THE WATER

The cruising cutter Foam, coast of Ireland, 3 June 1889
At 8.30am we left Glandore Harbour homeward bound. A fine day, a smooth sea, a nice little SW'ly breeze. Set course SE 3/4 S for the Longships, 156 miles away. We felt very sad as this beautiful country slowly faded from view. Surely there can be no finer cruising ground. A strong tidal stream runs around the headlands, but a mile or two outside them the tides are quite slack, in fact we never worried about the tides at all. There were many passing showers, but not one day of persistent rain. It is true that this coast is exposed to the whole drift of the Atlantic, but there is always a snug retreat to run for if the weather should prove too bad. And, unless the wind is due west, one generally has plenty of sheltered water to sail in.

Claud Worth, *Yacht Cruising*

William would have to redesign his pedalo many times before it became a commercial success.

THAT'S BIG

Sailors share the seas with all types of craft, and one of the biggest of them all is Hellesport Fairfax, or just Fairfax to her friends. When it comes to moving oil by sea, economies of scale mean that building big boats makes sense and Fairfax is a monster.

Built in South Korea, she is longer than six jumbo jets parked nose to tail and her rudder is bigger than a tennis court. She cost a whopping $65 million, but such is the demand for oil to be shipped from the Middle East to the US that she covered her building costs after just six trips. Fairfax can carry 3.2 million barrels of oil in 21 separate tanks, allowing her to transport different grades of crude oil without cross-contamination. Each tank is bigger than an Olympic-size swimming pool. After the oil is pumped out, special robotic showerheads descend into the tanks, cleaning them of any residue and readying them for the next load.

Fairfax is too big to pass through the Suez Canal, so has to take the long way round from Saudi Arabia to the US via the Cape of Good Hope at the southern tip of Africa. So if you're down that way and running low on oil, you may be lucky and come across the Hellesport Fairfax, which should be able to spare you a gallon or two.

Steel

Steel is heavy and steel is hard. It is this latter characteristic that makes it popular with sailors who will be venturing far from shore and a friendly boatyard. There are numerous tales of steel yachts hitting rocks, ships, whales, containers and all other manner of hard hazards and surviving the encounter with only a dent or two.

Steel's great strength comes at a price – weight. A heavy boat can be a slow boat, but with the right rig she need not be, and heavier boats should be more stable and capable of pushing through large seas. Rust is steel's other downside. It is preventable, but only through regular and thorough maintenance – especially inside the boat. If you build or buy a steel boat expect to spend a lot of time with a paintbrush, as bare steel is rust's best friend. On the other hand you can be sure that wherever you go there will be someone with a welding kit to carry out any repairs.

POINTS OF SAIL

The angle at which a boat is heading, relative to the direction of the wind, is known as the point of sail. There are five principal points of sail, from facing directly into the wind to having it dead astern.

Head-to-wind • Close-hauled
Close reach • Beam reach
Broad reach • Run

GOING DOWN

Boats are generally not designed to sink, but there are a few that make their living by doing exactly that. Biggest of them all is Mighty Servant, which her owners claim to be the strongest ship on the planet.

Mighty Servant earns her keep by carrying huge structures, such as oilrigs, across the world's oceans. Her cargo deck is 150m long and 50m wide and capable of carrying cargo weighing 45,000 tonnes. There is not a crane on the planet that could lift such a weight, so how does Mighty Servant get her cargo on board? By sinking.

This remarkable vessel has seacocks that can be opened, flooding ballast tanks with 70,000 tonnes of seawater. The accommodation section and bridge stay above the waves while the cargo deck sinks 22m below. Oilrigs and other giant, floating cargo can then be manoeuvred over the deck and held in place by tugs while Mighty Servant pumps out the ballast and slowly rises, lifting the cargo clear of the water. Piggyback, anyone?

70 *Number, in thousands, of beluga whales that are thought to be in the world's oceans*

Flying fish were now shooting up from under the bows, soaring for a moment then launching themselves again off the back of a wave with the stroke of their tails and soaring for another sixty feet or so. The spectacle was always new and we could watch it all morning, sitting on the foredeck hatch or standing in front of the windlass and holding the forestay so that we could see further. And we always watched with the same amazement these brilliant little playthings, like fan-shaped mirrors, who seemed to come up from under the bobstay.

'Françoise, a rainbow ... quick ... it will be gone in a minute ...'

With her chin on the cockpit coaming, hypnotised, Françoise looked for the first time in her life at this jewel suspended like an apparition in the fine spray of the bow-wave ... the Trade wind rainbow.

It played just above the bow-wave, disappeared, re-appeared, lit up, faded away and re-appeared again, threw out shafts of light and was gone.

I had occasionally seen momentary rainbows in the Mediterranean when Joshua was sailing in a mistral between Porquerolles and Corsica, miserable looking things in which the blue and yellow, watered down to a pale green, could hardly be distinguished from each other.

Only the miracle of the Trade wind could have produced a rainbow as radiant as the one we saw then. Maybe it is due to the particular limpidity of the tropical sky, or to the sun being so much higher and hotter than in the Northern latitudes. Perhaps it is also due to the special backcloth of the Trade wind sea. I don't know and it isn't important. I was simply happy that the Trade wind had presented Françoise with such a beautiful rainbow that day.

That richness of the colours varies a bit according to the angle at which the sun strikes the bow wave, and also depends on the quality of the particles of spray, spray which is as fine as mist. Under optimum conditions the rainbow at the bow can glow like a crown of jewels, and then the red appears, flashing like lightning. I mean the real red, the colour of blood, not merely orange tinted with red.

It is very rare to see the red. Much rarer than the green gleaming over the setting sun. I have seen the red only once, in the Indian Ocean on board Marie-Thérèse. It was like a blast from a trumpet, like looking into the heart of the Trade wind.

Bernard Moitessier, *Cape Horn – The Logical Route*

ROCK LIGHTHOUSES OF BRITAIN

**These marvels of engineering have been constructed in
these most testing of locations to keep mariners safe**

Eddystone, *Devon*
The Skerries, *Wales*
The Smalls, *Wales*
Longships, *Cornwall*
The Longstone, *Northumberland*
Bell Rock, *Scotland*
Skerryvore, *Scotland*
Bishop Rock, *Isles of Scilly*
Wolf Rock, *Cornwall*
Dubh Artach, *Scotland*
Chicken Rock, *Isle of Man*
Flannan Isles, *Scotland*

QUOTES ON BOATS

*Others may use the ocean as their road.
Only the English make it their abode.*
Edmund Walker, yachtsman and diplomat

THE MEDITERRANEAN MOOR

Not to be confused with Othello, the Moor of Venice, the Mediterranean moor is also complex and consists of different acts. There are relatively few marina berths or floating moorings in the Med and it is usual to moor your boat with her stern against the quayside, allowing you to step off the stern and into the nearest bar. Securing the back of the boat is easy; the tricky part is keeping the bows pointing out to sea. This is done by dropping the anchor as you approach the dockside in reverse. It's best to start reversing a long way out so that you have good control of the boat and can straighten up for the final approach. When about four boat-lengths from the quay, the order should be given to drop the anchor. Your crew must pay out the chain quickly to allow the yacht to continue its smooth backwards progress. Slowly approach the quay and give a blip of forward power at the last minute to stop the boat. A fender slung over the stern is a wise precaution. Lines are attached from the stern to the quay and the anchor chain can now be slowly hauled in to stop the bow swinging about.

It takes a little practice to master the Mediterranean moor and the fact that you are providing the entertainment for all the diners in the quayside tavernas does little to help the novice's nerves.

STEADY AS A... SHIP

Sailors go to sea for pleasure, and if they spend the voyage with their head over the side 'feeding the fishes', then they have no one to blame but themselves. Those for whom the sea is simply a place where they work can be more resentful of the motion of the ocean – especially if it stops them from getting on with their jobs. Scientists need a steady base from which to work more than most, so those fortunate enough to work on the Kilo Moana have no cause for complaint. Meaning 'One who seeks to understand the sea', Kilo Moana is a research vessel that spends long periods of time in the roughest parts of the North Pacific where the scientists that she carries study climate change.

Kilo Moana is a catamaran and maintains her steady footing among the shifting seas due to two torpedo-like pontoons that lie at the foot of each hull. These giant structures provide the buoyancy to lift the rest of the vessel above the breaking seas yet are deep enough not to be troubled by the rise and fall of the ocean swell. The sections of each hull that link the torpedoes to the superstructure are incredibly thin, offering the minimum of resistance to the waves and thus allowing the Kilo Moana to stay remarkably balanced. The technology is still in its infancy, but who knows, perhaps the day is not too far away when everyone who goes to sea will be sailing on an even keel.

THE REALITY OF SAILING

Electronics

Electronics make a sailor's life easier. At least that's the theory. In practice you go into a chandlery to be blinded by science and pay hundreds of pounds for a bit of kit that will be out of date in six months. Having got it on board, you realise that you'll have to drill dozens of holes in you bulkheads to mount the thing and all the wires are in the wrong place to connect it to your other kit. You run your engine for an hour to get enough power to start it (your other electronics have flattened your battery) and then attack the instructions booklet. The 'plug and play' promise does not come instantly true and you start to curse whoever translated the manual from Korean. You begin to get the hang of your kit but discover that it's not talking to your other onboard gizmos, which makes it virtually redundant. Your phone the helpline (calls are charged at £1.50 per minute) and eventually are told that you need to buy an extra cable that costs £20. You return to the chandlery, buy the cable, get back to the boat and plug it in. Everything works. You're ecstatic until you realise that the wind has died, the tide's gone out and it's started raining. You call it a day and head for home, wishing that you had gone sailing instead.

HOW TO ABANDON SHIP

Yachtsmen are told they should only step up into a life raft. This advice should not be taken literally, but it is true that a yacht should generally not be abandoned until she is definitely sinking. A damaged yacht still offers more shelter than a life raft, is more stable and is easier for rescuers to locate. If you are forced into it, a life raft will contain some safety equipment but, if time allows, take as much extra food, clothing and emergency supplies as is practical. Lash your dinghy to your life raft and use it to carry extra stores. Fill any suitable containers with fresh water to about three-quarters full, so that they will float. If you need glasses to read instructions (on flares, etc) have a spare pair in an emergency grab bag, along with vital medication and paperwork. Other items should include navigational gear, emergency beacons and transponders, and handheld VHFs.

NAUTICAL PHOBIAS

Irrational fears that may keep you away from the water

Ablutophobia	Fear of washing
Ancraophobia	Fear of wind
Bathophobia	Fear of depth
Bromidrosiphobia	Fear of body smells
Cymophobia	Fear of sea swell
Erythrophobia	Fear of port-hand markers
Homichlophobia	Fear of fog
Hydrophobia	Fear of the sea
Hygrophobia	Fear of dampness
Ichthyophobia	Fear of fish
Limnophobia	Fear of lakes
Potamophobia	Fear of rivers
Thalassophobia	Fear of the sea

A NAUTICAL JOKE

A sailor meets a pirate in a bar. The pirate has a peg leg, a hook and an eye patch. 'How'd you end up with a peg leg?' asks the sailor. 'I was swept overboard in a storm,' says the pirate. 'A shark bit off me whole leg.' 'Wow!' says the sailor. 'What about the hook?' 'We were boarding an enemy ship, battling the other seamen with swords. One of them cut me hand clean off.' 'Incredible!' remarks the sailor. 'And the eye patch?' 'A seagull dropping fell in me eye,' replies the pirate. 'You lost your eye to a seagull dropping?' the sailor asks incredulously. The pirate shrugs and replies: 'It was me first day with the hook.'

WORDS ON THE WATER

He always thought of the sea as *la mer* which is what people call her in Spanish when they love her. Sometimes those who love her say bad things of her but they are always said as though she were a woman. Some of the younger fishermen, those who used buoys as floats for their lines and had motorboats, bought when the shark livers had brought the money, spoke of her as *el mer* which is masculine. They spoke of her as a contestant or a place or even as an enemy. But the old man always thought of her as feminine and as something that gave or withheld great favours, and if she did wild or wicked things it was because she could not help them. The moon affects her as it does a woman, he thought.

Ernest Hemingway, *The Old Man and the Sea*

NAUTICAL PUZZLES

The good ship Saucy Sal sets sail from Eastport, bound for Westport, 26 miles away. She sails the most direct route and makes a steady nine knots over the ground. At the same time the equally good ship Naughty Nell sets sail from Westport, bound for Eastport. She too sails in a straight line but makes only six knots. How long will it be before the two ships meet?

Answer on page 153

PORT AND STARBOARD

Left and right will suffice for the man in the street, but at sea it must always be port and starboard. The word 'port', to mean 'left', is a relatively recent innovation, and the British and US navies only officially took it onboard in the nineteenth century. Prior to this, the opposite to 'starboard' was 'larboard', but the similarity between the two words meant that port got its big break.

The port side of any vessel will show a red light at night, while green lights are displayed to starboard. This helps you work out what other shipping is doing after the sun goes down, and is vital to avoid collisions.

If you have problems remembering that port is left and that red lights are shown on that side of a vessel, try to recall Mr Red who left port, or consider the fact that port is red and there is none left in the bottle. But don't feel bad if you can't remember – there are plenty of tales of captains of giant liners and admirals of aircraft carriers carrying slips of paper in their pockets on which are written simply: Port – left. Starboard – right.

Prior to the invention of modern foot pumps, small whales were often used to inflate rubber dinghies.

SAILING TERMS THAT
CONFUSE LANDLUBBERS

Knot

A knot is a knot, except at sea when it's not. Though it can be. Refer to a knot at sea and the sea dogs on board will presume you are talking about a measure of speed – one nautical mile per hour, to be precise. At sea the thing you make by tying a rope around itself or another rope is called by a specific name, such as a figure of eight or bowline. Ironically the original meaning of 'knot' became a victim of its own success. To work out a vessel's speed, a piece of wood was thrown overboard with a line attached. Knots were tied in the line at regular intervals and the rate with which they passed allowed you to calculate your speed. Knot a lot of people know that.

A Seagull outboard engine was once the only sort of outboard that any self-respecting sailor would be seen with. Clamped to the back of their dinghy, it would be used to propel them, quickly and efficiently, to their yacht. At least that was the idea. The reality was slightly different.

There now exists a generation of yachtsmen who know only the neat, light, clean and reliable outboards that come from Japan and Korea. None of these adjectives really suit the Seagull. Like their feathered namesakes, Seagulls were noisy and could be very messy. Their engineering was not hidden beneath a shiny plastic box but exposed for all to see. No quick pull of a chord to get a Seagull going. Oh no. Starting a Seagull involves a complex ritual that is passed down from father to son.

First a pull cord must be made. A bit of old rope with a knot in the end is best. The rope is then wound round the drum atop the engine. Next comes the fuel: a twist of the air valve on the fuel tank, a fiddle in the engine's bowels to open the fuel tap; a tickle of the tickler to draw fuel into the chamber; a wiggle of the choke depending on the weather, state of tide and general level of optimism. The throttle is then adjusted and only then can the chord be pulled.

But wait! One last part of the ritual must be completed – the warning. Anyone sitting in the dinghy stands a good chance of being hit in the face by the flying pull cord and so must be warned of the imminent start. This gives them the chance to then turn their backs to the mighty Seagull and cower – hopefully keeping their vital organs out of harm's way.

Now the pull. The starter (generally the strongest person on board) makes sure the drum is wound tight then gives an almighty heave. If he falls over and the engine does not start (which is usually the case), the starter clambers then to his feet again and starts the whole process over again. Perhaps a little less choke this time and a touch more throttle. Wind up the drum. Warn crew. Pull!

If Neptune is smiling, the Seagull will roar into life, shattering the calm of the waterside and you will be on your way. Until the propeller becomes fouled with weed, that is. To clear it, the engine has to be tipped forward so that the revolving propeller breaks the water's surface and spins madly in the air, thus throwing both water and weed over everyone.

They just don't make outboards like that any more.

FAMOUS WATERY DEATHS

People who should have stayed away from boats
– or water in general

Jeff Buckley *Pop star*
Drowned

Donald Crowhurst
Famous yachtsman
Presumed to have 'stepped
overboard'

Harold Holt
Australian PM
Drowned

Lord Lucan
Alleged murderer
Presumed drowned
mid-Channel

Kirsty MacColl *Pop star*
Killed in a jet ski accident

Robert Maxwell *Media mogul*
Drowned after falling overboard

Angus Primrose *Yacht designer*
Lost overboard

Percy Shelley *Poet*
Drowned while sailing off Italy

Eric Tabarly *Famous yachtsman*
Lost overboard

Natalie Wood *Actress*
Fell overboard while securing
the tender

Virginia Woolf *Author*
Drowned herself in the
River Ouse

QUOTES ON BOATS

*One sight [of Cape Horn] is enough to make a landsman
dream for a week about death, peril, and shipwreck*
Charles Darwin, naturalist

SNUFF'S ENOUGH

There were fortunes to be made at sea during the seventeenth and eighteenth centuries, and naval warfare and piracy were both constants. Victory was normally decided by the skill with which a ship was handled, the direction of the wind or the strength of a ship's firepower – however, in 1702, a naval engagement was decided by a cargo of snuff.

The English Navy was attacking the French and Spanish fleets, and things didn't look good for one of the English ships that had been set on fire by a enemy fireship. Fortunately the fireship had a cargo of snuff which blew up with such force that the blast extinguished the flames onboard the English vessel. A witness recorded that: 'It so affected the crews of the French warships that many of them had to dive into the sea for relief from the pain of having inhaled the snuff.'

78 *Percentage of yachtsmen who said, in a recent survey, that for them
sailing was a form of escapism*

INTERNATIONAL FLAG CODES

**There is a different flag for every letter in the alphabet,
and each, when flown alone, has a specific meaning.**

A	Diver below (when stationary); I am undergoing a speed trial
B	I am taking on or discharging explosives
C	Yes (affirmative)
D	Keep clear of me, I am manoeuvring with difficulty
E	I am altering my course to starboard
F	I am disabled, communicate with me
G	I require a pilot
H	I have a pilot on board
I	I am altering my course to port
J	I am going to send a message by semaphore
K	You should stop your vessel instantly
L	You should stop, I have something important to communicate
M	I have a doctor on board
N	No (negative)
O	Man overboard
P	The Blue Peter – all aboard, vessel is about to proceed to sea. At sea: your lights are out or burning badly
Q	My vessel is healthy and I request free practique (permission to travel freely)
R	The way is off my ship (I am not moving). You may feel your way past me
S	My engines are going full speed astern
T	Do not pass ahead of me
U	You are standing (moving) into danger
V	I require assistance (not distress)
W	I require medical assistance
X	Stop carrying out your intentions and watch for my signals
Y	I am carrying mail
Z	To be used to address or call shore stations

CRUISING COCKTAILS

Sex on the Beach

This cocktail is well named, as, like the real thing, it sounds like a good idea at the time but can leave you sore in the morning if you overindulge.

Take a long glass (or an old orange mug if you are on a gaff-rigged yacht) and throw in some ice if you have it. Add a healthy tot of vodka and an equal quantity of peach schnapps. Top up with fresh orange juice and cranberry juice – watch out for the pips. A couple of crushed raspberries finishes it all off. Rinse everything well afterwards to clean off any seeds that have not been swallowed.

HOW TO FILLET A MACKEREL

No fish are easier to catch from a sailing boat than mackerel. Nearly every yacht has a mackerel line with spinners or feathered hooks to snare these most British of fish. Simply unwind the line from the stern, make sure you don't sail too fast, wait for 10 minutes and reel in the line. Repeat until you get lucky – it rarely takes long.

Once you have the fish on board, you'll need to kill them. Different people adopt different techniques, but a quick blow to the head with a winch handle often does the trick. Once good and dead, the head can be cut off and the fish gutted. To do this, insert a knife in the bottom of the fish near the tail, and draw forwards. Scoop everything out from the cavity you have revealed and rinse the mackerel.

You are now faced with two choices: cooking or eating raw.

The latter option may not immediately appeal, but think about it. You will rarely be able to eat sushi as fresh as this. If you don't have soy sauce, wasabi and pickled ginger to hand, you may decide to cook the fish. A bit of butter in a frying pan is all you need, although if you want to add a element of sophistication, you can fillet the fish first by running a knife along the spine from tail to head. Smoking your fillets is a delicious alternative to frying them. Portable fish smokers can be bought for about £50 and, armed with some methylated spirit to create the heat and sawdust to make the smoke, you can make your own smoked mackerel fillets in a matter of minutes, and they taste infinitely better than the shrink-wrapped versions sold in supermarkets.

WORDS ON THE WATER

They that go down to the sea in ships, that do business in great waters;
    These see the works of the Lord, and his wonders in the deep.
    For he commandeth, and raiseth the stormy wind, which lifteth up the waves thereof,
    They mount up to the heaven they go down again to the depths; their soul is melted because of trouble.
    They reel to and fro, and stagger like a drunken man, and are at their wit's end.
    Then they cry unto the Lord in their trouble, and he bringeth them out of their distresses.
    He maketh the strum a calm, so that the waves thereof are still.
    Then are they glad because they be quiet; so he bringeth them unto their desired haven.

Psalm 107

The world's largest seas and oceans

		Square kilometres	Square miles
1.	Pacific Ocean	166,242,500	64,186,600
2.	Atlantic Ocean	86,557,800	33,420,160
3.	Indian Ocean	73,427,800	28,350,640
4.	Arctic Ocean	13,223,800	5,105,740
5.	South China Sea	2,974,600	1,148,499
6.	Caribbean Sea	2,515,900	971,400
7.	Mediterranean Sea	2,510,000	969,120
8.	Bering Sea	2,261,100	873,020
9.	Sea of Okhotsk	1,527,570	589,800
10.	Gulf of Mexico	1,507,600	582,100

The Pacific Ocean accounts for 46% of all the water on Earth, the Atlantic Ocean 23.9% and the Indian Ocean 20.3%.

QUOTES ON BOATS

'Twas them days a ship was part of the sea, and a man was part of the ship, and the sea joined all together and made it one.
Eugene O'Neill, playwright

TWINKLE, TWINKLE

There are few experiences as magical as sailing through a sea that is alight with phosphorescence. This most remarkable of natural phenomena is caused by biochemical reactions in a variety of sea creatures. There are some fish that can turn their lights on and off, drawing prey to them or scaring attackers away. However, the lights one most often sees when sailing come from tiny animals and occur when the water is disturbed by waves or a yacht's wake. A dolphin swimming in such waters becomes an illuminated torpedo or an underwater firework. Such 'disturbed water luminescence' is sometimes seen around British shores but is more common in warmer climates and is not the only type of phosphorescence. Parts of the Arabian Sea sometimes give off a constant, even white glow known as the Milky Sea. Mariners throughout the years have described beams of light moving quickly over the waters of the Indian Ocean and the China Sea. Official Admiralty publications also include descriptions of 'luminous masses apparently coming to the surface and exploding' to light up a large area, as well as flashing patches and areas of light that apparently expand and contract.

SEAGULLS

Seagulls sometimes like to dry their little seagull bottoms and have a bit of a waddle after a swim. Unfortunately they do not confine their waddling to the seashore or the local council tip, but also settle on yachts' decks – and seagulls are not fussy about where they go to the loo. Leave your boat for a couple of weeks and you will probably return to find her decks encrusted in guano, which takes an age to scrub away.

Sailors spend a lot of time and money keeping seagulls and their droppings off their decks. Some tie carrier bags on pieces of string from the boom, these flutter in the wind and look horrible to seagulls and other yachtsmen. Others laboriously crisscross their decks with tape, preventing the birds from settling at all. CDs are hung from the rigging of some yachts, though whether seagulls are more averse to Barry Manilow than Britney Spears is not yet known. If things get desperate you can buy a bird scarer that will either go bang every few minutes, or replicate the sound of a hungry hawk about to descend from the skies for a seagull snack. Neither audible option is likely to prove popular with neighbouring yachts. Keeping a fox, ferret or cat on board does work, though there are animal cruelty issues involved, so make your choice carefully.

SEA SAYINGS

Slush fund

Ship's cooks supplemented their meagre wages by selling on the fat from salted meat storage barrels. This slush was sought after by candle makers and provided the cook with valuable extra income.

SAILING CLASSES PROPOSED
FOR THE 2008 OLYMPICS

Multihull Open: Tornado
Keelboat Women: Yngling
Keelboat Men: Star
Double-handed Dinghy Open: 49er
Double-handed Dinghy Women: 470
Double-handed Dinghy Men: 470
Single-handed Dinghy Men: Finn
Single-handed Dinghy Open: Laser
Single-handed Dinghy Women: Laser Radial
Windsurfer Men: Neil Pryde RS-X
Windsurfer Women: Neil Pryde RS-X

NOXIOUS LIQUID SUBSTANCES

Merchant shipping regulations identify four types of Noxious Liquid Substances (NLS). Discharges of them into the sea are prohibited.

Category A
Present a major hazard to either marine resources or human health and justify the application of stringent anti-pollution measures

Category B
Present a hazard to either marine resources or human health and justify the application of special anti-pollution measures

Category C
Present a minor hazard to either marine resources or human health and require special operational conditions

Category D
Present a major hazard to either marine resources or human health and require some attention in operational conditions

QUOTES ON BOATS

It is all so clear why ships, sailing ships, over the centuries have always been referred to as 'she'. The rounded form of their hulls with the subtle blend of one soft curve into another with no hard masculine lines. And above all the smooth, full-bodied shape of the sails pushing outwards like the bodice of a lovely woman. A ship has to be feminine.
Ben Pester, Cape Horner

TIME FOR A NAP?

If there's one thing you need a lot of when single-handing a 60ft racing yacht around the world, it's sleep. However, with your fellow yachtsmen pushing their boats hard, there can be no respite – take your foot off the gas, so to speak, and you'll be passed. If you're asleep, you can't be getting the most from your boat and reacting to every wind shift and wave.

If this is your problem, take a tip from Ellen MacArthur, Britain's leading single-handed yachtswoman. When she set off round the world in the Vendée Globe in 2000, she knew that she had to sleep as little as possible yet still be mentally and physically fit enough to cope with the challenges that the oceans would throw at her. Her solution was to catch snatches of sleep at intervals throughout the day. During her 94-day voyage she slept 891 times – but her average time asleep was just 36 minutes.

I THINK I'LL BUILD MY BOAT WITH...

Glass Reinforced Plastic

Glass Reinforced Plastic, or GRP, revolutionised the boat building industry in the 1960s and 1970s. The vast majority of modern yachts are built from this strong, versatile, cheap and easily shaped material. GRP's greatest attraction is the fact that it more or less looks after itself. Unlike wood it will not rot, and unlike steel it will not rust, though it does not have the same ability to withstand knocks as some other materials.

Osmosis, or the dreaded boat pox, is GRP's Achilles' heel. Air spaces in the hull draw in water, causing the holes to grow bigger, weakening the structure of the boat. It is a problem in some older boats but is now rare and many yachts that used to suffer have been successfully treated. If you don't have a huge amount of time or money and don't plan to voyage far from a boatyard, then GRP is almost certainly for you.

NAUTICAL PUZZLES

You need to make a new mast for your yacht and see a perfectly shaped tree trunk sticking out of the riverbed. You know that one-half of the pole is in the ground, another one-third of it is covered by water, and 11ft is out of the water. What is the total length of the pole in feet?
Answer on page 153

WORDS ON THE WATER

The American Brig, Commerce, Atlantic Ocean, south of the Azores, 14 April 1798.
Saw a vessel at break of day, and soon perceived she was in chase of us. We made all sail we could, but about 9 o'clock she came up and gave us a gun. I then hove our main topsail to the mast, and showed our colours. The captain ordered me to hoist out my boat and come on board, with my papers, which I did. She proved to be the French [*privateer*] La Revenge, Capt Grallet, of 16 guns from Bordeaux. He immediately hoisted out his boat and

sent on board the Commerce, but they returned with only plundering a few boxes of raisins, fruit &c. The captain then ordered a research by different officers, who, after digging in the salt about two hours, discovered 22 jars, in which were 11,000 dollars, the property of Messrs Murray and Mumford, and John and RB Forbes, of New York. I was then stripped in the privateer's cabin, even to my shirt and robbed of money to the amount of 160 dollars in gold, belonging to Mr Benj B Mumford.
Captain John B Thurston

A STAR TO GUIDE ME

Some of the stars visible in the northern hemisphere that are used for traditional navigation

Altair • Ddeneb • Mirfak

Aldeebaran • Rigel

Bellatrix • Alnilam • Elnath

• Capella • Procyon

Arcturus • Vega • Alkaid

Alioth • Spica • Regulus

Dubhe • Rasalhague

SHIP IN DISTRESS

A few distress signals that may be heard or seen at sea

- A gun or other explosive device fired at intervals of about a minute.
- Continuous sounding of any fog-signal apparatus.
- Rockets or shells, throwing red stars, fired one at a time, at short intervals.
- A signal made by radiotelephony or by any other signalling method consisting of the group --- − − − --- ('SOS' in Morse code).
- A signal sent by radiotelephony consisting of the spoken word 'mayday'.
- The international code of signals (normally flags) for distress indicated by 'NC'.
- A signal consisting of a square flag having above or below it a ball, or anything resembling a ball.
- Flames on the vessel (as from a burning tar barrel, oil barrel, etc).
- A rocket parachute flare or hand flare showing a red light.
- A smoke signal giving off orange-coloured smoke.
- Slowly and repeatedly raising and lowering arms outstretched to each side.
- The radiotelegraph alarm signal (12 four-second dashes per minute set at one-second intervals).
- The radiotelephone alarm signal (alternate tones of 1300Hz and 220Hz transmitted on 2182kHz for a period of 30 to 60 seconds).
- Signals transmitted by Emergency Position-Indicating Radio Beacons (EPIRBs).
- Approved signals transmitted by radio communications systems, allowing the full range of marine distress equipment to be employed.
- Standing naked in a life raft in the middle of the Pacific Ocean, shouting 'Help!' and waving your arms madly. (Unofficial, but effective.)

QUOTES ON BOATS

It is as hard to describe the fascination of the sea as to explain the beauty of a woman, for, to each man, either it is self-evident, or no argument can help him see it.
Claud Worth, yachtsman

UNIDENTIFIED FLOATING OBJECTS

While oilrigs can be a hazard to sailors, rising up out of the deep blue sea, at least they are anchored to the seabed. The same cannot be said of semi-submersible rigs – huge mobile structures that can propel themselves across the world's oceans, searching for oil and gas deep beneath the sea. The biggest of these is Eric Raude, named after a Viking – Eric the Red. For $150,000 a day you can charter Eric to comb the North Atlantic, searching for some of the estimated 78 trillion cubic feet of gas that are believed to lie there, as yet undiscovered.

Eric is propelled by a series of Rolls-Royce thrusters, the biggest ever built, which are linked to satellite navigation systems. When she is over the spot to be drilled, the thrusters constantly balance her position to counter wind, waves and currents. When the drilling is finished they can swivel to face in the same direction and drive the rig through the sea to her next destination.

Eric was built to cope with conditions in what her captain describes as 'the meanest, roughest, toughest place to work'. The storms of the North Atlantic are some of the most ferocious on the planet, as proved by the loss of the semi-submersible Ocean Ranger in a storm prior to Eric's launch. No one survived that tragedy, which caused designers to rethink how semi-submersibles should be built. Eric has subsequently made it through three 'hundred-year storms' – the sort that normally come only once a century – and her crew have grown to trust her.

So if you're sailing along and start to question your sanity when you see an oilrig moving with no sign of a tug, don't worry, it's probably only Eric the Red.

WORDS ON THE WATER

Let your boat of life be light, packed with only what you need – a homely home and simple pleasures, one or two friends, worth the name, someone to love and someone to love you, a cat, a dog, and a pipe or two, enough to eat and enough to wear, and a little more than enough to drink; for thirst is a dangerous thing.
Jerome K Jerome, *Three Men in a Boat*

'Strewth captain! Look at that for a poor bit of parking.'

RACING FOR PLEASURE

Sailors have always tried to sail their boats as fast as possible. For many years the drive behind this need for speed was purely commercial. The sooner you reached the fishing grounds or trading port, the sooner you could catch your fish or sell your cargo and keep the captain happy. But men are naturally competitive and wherever there are two similar sailing boats, there is likely to be some sort of race taking place. The first documented race of modern times took place in 1661 when King Charles raced his brother, the Duke of York, on a course from Greenwich to Gravesend. The King won and yacht racing has never looked back since.

THE OLDEST YACHT CLUBS
IN THE WORLD

Flotilla of the Neva, *Russia, 1718*
Royal Cork Yacht Club, *Ireland, 1720*
Lough Ree Yacht Club, *Ireland, 1770*
Starcross Yacht Club, *UK, 1772*
Royal Thames Yacht Club, *England, UK, 1775*
Royal Yacht Squadron, *UK, 1815*
Republic of Singapore Yacht Club, *Singapore, 1826*
Royal Western Yacht Club of England, *UK, 1827*
Royal Swedish Yacht Club, *Sweden, 1830*
Royal Irish Yacht Club, *Ireland, 1831*
Lough Derg Yacht Club, *Ireland, 1835*
Royal Eastern Yacht Club, *UK, 1835–1969*
Royal Malta Yacht Club, *Malta, 1835*
Royal Nova Scotia Yacht Squadron, *Canada, 1837*
Royal Southern Yacht Club, *UK, 1837*
Tamar Yacht Club, *Australia, 1837*
Deben Yacht Club, *UK, 1838*
Royal St George Yacht Club, *Ireland, 1838*
Royal Perth Yacht Club, *Australia, 1841*
Societé des Retates du Havre, *France, 1842*
Royal Harwich Yacht Club, *UK, 1843*
Royal Bermuda Yacht Club, *Bermuda, 1844*
Royal Victoria Yacht Club, *UK, 1845*
Royal Bombay Yacht Club, *India, 1846*
Royal Netherlands Yacht Club, *The Netherlands, 1847*
Royal Row & Sailing Society, *1851*
Poole Yacht Club, *UK, 1852*
Royal Canadian Yacht Club, *Canada, 1852*
Royal Yacht Club of Victoria, *Australia, 1853*
Goolwa Regatta Yacht Club, *Australia, 1854*
Associacao Naval de Lisboa, *Portugal 1856*
Ranelagh Yacht Club, *UK, about 1857*
Royal Temple Yacht Club, *UK 1857*
Royal Natal Yacht Club, *South Africa 1858*
Royal Geelong Yacht Club, *Australia, 1859*
Royal New Zealand Yacht Squadron, *New Zealand, 1859*
Royal Norfolk & Suffolk Yacht Club, *UK, 1859*
St Petersburg River Yacht Club, *Russia, 1860*
Nylandska Jaktklubben, *Finland, 1861*
Yacht Club de Quebec, *Canada, 1861*
Holywood Yacht Club, *N Ireland, 1862*
Royal Channel Islands Yacht Club, *UK, 1862*
Royal Sydney Yacht Squadron, *Australia, 1862*

SAILING STEREOTYPES

The yacht club committee member

Yacht clubs rely on their members to run many aspects of the club's administration and there are numerous committees. Some of these are efficient decision-making organisations with members who realise that sitting on the Post Race Recreation Sub Committee of Little Mudling YC is not the same thing as being an international delegate at the United Nations. Others sadly do not, and use their participation in these committee meetings to try and add some meaning to what may otherwise be somewhat meaningless lives. As a committee member they have power and they will wield it. Absolute power may corrupt absolutely, but trivial power corrupts infuriatingly.

A quick vote is needed on whether to give ham and cheese sandwiches or sausage rolls to the mid-week racers – the chairman tries to whisk proceedings along, but our committee man is not having any of it. These things must be done properly. That's how they did it when he was in business, etc. Committee man has nowhere better to go, so is happy for the meeting to go on all night; his fellow sailors around the table are powerless while he bangs on and on.

He thinks he'd make a great commodore, but for some reason no one ever proposes him.

QUOTES ON BOATS

No man should be a sailor who has enough contrivance to get himself into jail, for being at sea is like being in jail with the added possibility of being drowned.
Dr Johnson, scholar

THE AULD MUG

The America's Cup, dating from 1851, is considered by some to be the oldest trophy in international sport. No prize money is awarded to the winner, yet racing syndicates spend tens of millions of dollars mounting campaigns to either defend or challenge for the America's Cup and prove their technological supremacy at sea.

The cup itself, known as the Auld Mug, is 26 inches tall and made from 134 ounces of silver-plated Britannia metal (similar to pewter). It was crafted by R&G Garrard, Queen's jewellers, in London, in about 1848. The cup was made for the Royal Yacht Squadron as a yacht racing trophy and was originally dubbed the 100 Guinea Cup. A seven-inch base was added to the America's Cup in 1958 to accommodate the additional winners' names.

BEYOND THE HORIZON

Excitement and adventure always lie beyond the horizon, but just how far is that? Well it all depends how tall you are and how far above sea level you are standing. The rough rule is to increase the square root of the number of feet that the eye is above sea level by one third of itself. The result will be the distance of the horizon in miles. If that seems like hard work you can use this table:

Height above sea level (feet)	Distance to horizon (miles)
5	2.9
20	5.9
50	9.3
100	13.2
500	29.5
1,000	41.6
2,000	58.9
5,000	93.1

QUOTES ON BOATS

I think, as far as yachting is concerned, there is not a blasted thing about the whole blooming game that is half as good as it used to be.
L Francis Herreshoff, yacht designer and author

CRUISING COCKTAILS

Rum Punch
When in Rome do as the Romans, and when sailing in the Caribbean, drink rum punch. For the yachtsman, no drink is as closely linked to a place as is rum punch and the clear blue seas and fresh winds of the Caribbean.

There are as many ways to make this classic cocktail as there are delightful anchorages and sleepy ports, and as long as it tastes great and gets you dancing, no one will complain. If in doubt, stick to this basic formula:

One of sour
Two of sweet
Three of strong
And four of weak

The sour is normally lime juice, though some add bitters too. The sweet is sugar syrup, but pineapple and orange juice often appear. The strong has to be rum, of which there is rarely a shortage, and the weak can be anything from water to more juice.

WINTER CHECKLIST

Taking your boat out of the water for the winter? Don't forget to:

Clean fuel filters
Change the oil
Add antifreeze to coolants
Remove the impeller
Coat battery terminals in Vaseline
Take all sails down
Secure halyards
Ventilate the boat
Clean the heads
Grease the seacocks
Check for osmosis

– and make a note of all the jobs you've done so you
don't do them again in the spring

WORDS ON THE WATER

Oh, early in the morning
A sailor likes his baccy O!
A packet of twist
And a packet of shag
And a packet of Yankee-doodle O!
Oh, early in the morning
A sailor likes his baccy O!

Traditional shanty

THE FASTNET RACE

In 1925, 14 yachts raced from the Solent, down the English Channel and around the Fastnet Rock off Ireland, finishing in Plymouth. There was debate at the time as to whether such an Ocean Race (as it was known) was a safe and sensible thing to do. That first race was won by Jolie Brise in six days and three hours, and the event soon became a famous fixture in the yachting calendar.

Fame turned to infamy in 1979 when the fleet of the Fastnet race was caught out by a storm in the Atlantic. The racing yachts of the day simply could not cope with the horrendous conditions. Of the 303 yachts that started the race, 23 were abandoned or sunk. Of the 2,500 sailors who took part, 136 were rescued. Fifteen people died. The race is still held every year but the Fastnet disaster has had a massive impact on the design of ocean-going boats, and the quantity and design of safety equipment they must now carry.

THE EARLY YEARS OF THE RNLI

1824	Sir William Hillary, a courageous lifeboatman, coordinates the first lifeboat service. His appeal to the nation leads to the foundation of the National Institution for the Preservation of Life from Shipwreck, later to become the RNLI. Also the year in which the Gold Medal for outstanding bravery was founded.
1830	Sir William Hillary receives a Gold Medal for his part in the rescue of the crew of the St George.
1839	The number of lifeboat stations around Britain reaches 30.
1840	Early rescues are made using the Manby rocket.
1843	The 50th dedicated lifeboat is launched in Cromer.
1849	Lives saved total 6,716.
1854	Captain Ward, an RNLI Inspector, invents a cork lifejacket, which gives lifeboat crews weather protection as well as buoyancy.
1854	The Institution changes its name to the Royal National Lifeboat Institution.

WHAT A SUPERYACHT

There are yachts and then there are superyachts. There is no precise way of defining whether you are looking at a big yacht or a superyacht, except that if you need to ask the question then it's not a superyacht. These are the boats that the rich and famous use as mobile apartments and luxury playthings. They'll be kept in the Mediterranean for the summer then taken to the Caribbean to cruise beneath the winter sun.

Superyachts need not have sails, though more and more luxury craft are being built that combine the opulence of a gin palace with the some of the style that can only come with a boat that can be driven by her sails alone. These vessels are incredibly expensive to build and often their super-rich owners are too busy either making money or spending it to make much use of them. So they remain on standby, their crew keeping them perpetually polished in case the owner's Ferrari roars into the marina.

If you lack the millions but fancy the lifestyle, why not sign up as crew on a superyacht? The hours can be long and the owners can be demanding but you get to travel the world in luxury and will have the boat to yourself for long stretches. You can play with all the toys onboard – jet-skis, windsurfers, etc – and don't have to pay any tax on your generous salary.

If this sounds like the life for you, it's best to get as many sailing or motorboat qualifications as possible before heading to the sun, doing the rounds of the marinas and hoping your boat comes in.

'You couldn't have a look at my rudder mounting while you're down there?' King Arthur asked tentatively.

SAILING TERMS THAT CONFUSE LANDLUBBERS

Clew

Tell your skipper that you haven't a clue and he'll probably agree. Tell him that you haven't a clew and he'll tell you to bloody well find one and tie a rope to it. The clew is the outside bottom (or 'aft lower', in sailing speak) corner of a sail, to which is attached the sheets that control the sail. The sheets are ropes that run through blocks, though the blocks are not blocks at all. Instead of being square, as a block should be, they are mostly round, to allow ropes to pass smoothly through them, and are used to lead the sheets towards the stern – but don't let the name fool you, some sterns can be very jolly places.

LASER POWER

When it first appeared in 1969, the Laser dinghy revolutionised dinghy sailing, and it is still going strong. Although more than 30 years old, it is still the dinghy of choice for many sailors, combining simplicity and speed. More than 100,000 have been built and there are competitive fleets of them in every corner of the world. The Laser is an Olympic class dinghy and with its 76 square feet of sail can be a demanding boat to sail. Fortunately the original Laser now has numerous brothers and sisters allowing all sorts of people to enjoy Laser sailing.

Laser	Single-handed adult
Laser Radial	Single-handed small adult, women and youth
Laser 4.7	Single-handed small youth
Laser Pico	One adult/two adults/adult-child/two or three children
Laser Funboat	One adult/adult-child/two children
Laser 2 Regatta	Two-person adult racing
Laser Vortex	Single-handed adult
Laser 2000	Two adult – two adult/two children
Laser 4000	Two-person adult racing
Laser Stratos	For all the family
Laser SB3	3 person adult

NAUTICAL PUZZLES

Rearrange this phrase to discover a nautical command:
Headlands clonk
Answer on page 153

THREE PEAKS

There is something slightly masochistic about going sailing. Unless you are on a luxury liner, there will be certain privations that must be endured when at sea. Some tolerate these little hardships, others enjoy them but some people still find the whole thing still too easy. It was for these people that Bill Tilman devised the Three Peaks Race.

Tilman was a mountaineer and yachtsman and the race reflects his twin passions. Yachts starts at Barmouth in mid-Wales and sail 62 miles to Caernarfon. Two members of the crew are put ashore and set off on the 24-mile round trip to the top of Snowdon, Wales' highest mountain. There follows a 92-mile voyage to Ravenglass and the ascent of Scafell Pike, England's loftiest peak, and a 32-mile hike. Fort William, 235 nautical miles away, is the next port of call from where Ben Nevis must be scaled. The 17-mile slog involves a climb of over 4,000ft. The first crew back from this climb wins the race.

And we pumped. And there was no break in the weather. The sea was white like a sheet of foam, like a cauldron of boiling milk; there was not a break in the clouds, no – not the size of a man's hand – no, not for so much as ten seconds. There was for us no sky, there were for us no stars, no sun, no universe – nothing but angry clouds and an infuriated sea. We pumped watch and watch for dear life; and it seemed to last for months, for years, for all eternity, as though we had been dead and gone to a hell for sailors. We forgot the day of the week, the name of the month, what year it was, and whether we had ever been ashore.

The sails blew away, she lay broadside on under a weather cloth, the ocean poured over her, and we did not care. We turned those handles, and had the eyes of idiots. As soon as we had crawled on deck I used to take a turn with the rope around the men, the pumps, and the mainmast, and we turned, we turned incessantly, with the water to our waists, to our necks, over our heads. It was all one, we had forgotten how it felt to be dry.

Joseph Conrad, *Youth*

EMERGENCY SUPPLIES

What you can expect to find in a typical offshore life raft

Oars • Bailer • Repair kit
Flashlight • Spare batteries
Jack knife • Flares, handheld
Hand pump • Water packets
Rations • Water storage bag
Fishing kit • Sponge • Signal mirror
First aid kit • Seasickness tablets
Survival manual • SOLAS parachute flare

SUBMARINE SAFETY

There have been several incidents when fishing vessels and even yachts have disappeared at sea and submarines have been thought to be responsible. If you are worried about submarine accidents you should run your engine or generator, even when under sail, and keep your echo sounder switched on. You should also show deck-level navigation lights at night on the pulpit and stern. It is common sense to stay clear of charted submarine exercise areas and away from any vessel flying code flags 'NE2' meaning that submarines are in the vicinity. Subfacts – warnings of planned or known submarine activity – are broadcast by local coastguard stations.

QUOTES ON BOATS

*Relive the experience of sailing by standing under
a cold shower, ripping up £20 notes.*
Anon

RAGGIE OR STINKPOT?

It's commonly believed (by those who stay ashore) that a camaraderie exists among those who go to sea – but nothing could be further from the truth. The sad fact is that there are as many divisions, rivalries, prejudices and snobberies at sea as there are on land. It is a minefield for anyone new to boating, but there are some basic rules.

First, anyone who is paid to go out to sea has little time or respect for those who do so for pleasure. A fisherman is pleased to see a yacht only if it has lost its mast and is about to be washed on to the rocks. The fisherman wishes no harm on the crew, he merely wants to be able to tow the yacht to safety and claim thousands of pounds of salvage.

The crew of supertankers and container ships have even less regard for the leisure sailor. Yachtsmen may think that power gives way to sail, but it takes four miles to slow down a supertanker and they're working to strict timetables. Arrive in port late and they'll miss serious drinking time. They are not going to stop for some fool with a sail – especially as the bridge is probably unmanned and the radar set to go 'bleep' only if it picks up another ship that could do it damage – not an eminently crunchable yacht.

The yachtsman has his own enemies; while he may be looked down on by the fisherman and ignored by commercial shipping, at least he is not a motorboater – or so he tells himself. Motorboats, or 'stinkpots' as he likes to call them, are considered vulgar by the majority of yachtsmen. They shatter the sailing serenity, kick up a huge wake that spills the yachtsman's coffee and are frequently owned by men with tattoos. Imagine! The fact that these vulgar fellows' boats cost 10 times more than most yachts has nothing to do with this sailing snobbery. Perish the thought.

Of course the motorboaters do not take this lying down – and nor do their trophy wives. Instead they invite each other over for a drink and chuckle about the stupidity of yachtsmen – or 'raggies', as they call them. Yachts are tippy, uncomfortable, clearly dangerous and spend half the time motoring anyway. 'So I drive a stinkpot, do I?' a motorboater asks with a laugh. 'Well at least I'm not a WAFI*!' And he and his friends all fall about.

*Wind Assisted F*****g Idiot

SAY IT WITH FLAGS

You can say a lot at sea just by hoisting a couple of flags. Here are some signals that the Navy will recognise:

C R
Is the sea smooth enough to alight near you?

E X
Bar is dangerous

J K
I am swinging or about to swing

O L
Heave-to or I will open fire on you

P Q
I have sprung a leak

T K
I require provisions urgently

And some they might not:

L O
Ahoy!

P P
I am emptying my tanks

G T
I require ice and a lemon

I I
Affirmative

B O
Do not anchor downwind of me

Year in the fifteenth century that John Cabot became the first man to sail from 97 England across the Atlantic

FIND THE COMFY SPOT

There is, in every cockpit, a perfect place to sit. This will vary from boat to boat and will also vary according to the angle at which she is sailing. Most cockpits are comfortable in harbour, but when the yacht starts to heel, you suddenly find that you've got a winch in your back or that the mainsail traveller is threatening to slice off your fingers, or worse. You need somewhere to settle, with good support, out of the worst of the weather and where you won't get in the way. The three favourite spots are:

1. Huddled with your back to the cabin bulkhead, looking astern and out of the wind.

2. Right at the stern, in one corner or the other. You should be safe from spray here and can nestle against the pushpit – considerably more comfortable than the wires of the guardrails further forward.

3. The companionway. Everyone seems to be drawn to the stairs at a party and it is the same on yachts. Standing on the steps down to the cabin allows you to see what is going on, and feel part of it all, without putting your boots on. However, just as at a party, such stair dwellers get in the way of those trying to get past and you'll eventually be moved on – although it won't be long before someone takes your place.

WORDS ON THE WATER

King Erik of Sweden was in his time held second to none in the magical art; and he was so familiar with the evil spirits whom he worshipped that what waysoever he turned his cap, the wind would presently blow that way. For this he was called Windycap.

Olaus Magnus, *Description of the Northern Peoples*

NAVAL TOASTS

Monday	Our ships at sea
Tuesday	Our men
Wednesday	Ourselves
Thursday	A bloody war or a sickly season
Friday	A willing foe and sea room
Saturday	Sweethearts and wives (may they never meet)
Sunday	Absent friends

Thursday's toast harks back to the days when promotion came only on the death of a superior officer. Friday's toast stems from the fact that success in battles meant a share of the bounty for the commanding officers.

QUOTES ON BOATS

*Men in a ship are always looking up, and men ashore
generally looking down.*
John Masefield, poet and novelist

THE QUARTERMASTER'S STORES

**Here is the traditional sailor's ditty in full –
ideal for long boat journeys**

*There were rats, rats, big as blooming cats,
In the stores, in the stores.
There were rats, rats, big as blooming cats,
In the quartermaster's stores.
My eyes are dim, I cannot see,
I have not got my specs with me,
I have not got my specs with me.*

**Depending on the length of your journey, you
might need the rest of the verses...**

Mice ... *running through the rice*
Snakes ... *as big as garden rakes*
Beans ... *as big as submarines*
Gravy ... *enough to float the navy*
Cakes ... *that give us tummy aches*
Eggs ... *with scaly chicken legs*
Butter ... *running in the gutter*
Lard ... *they sell it by the yard*
Bread ... *with great big lumps like lead*
Cheese ... *that makes you want to sneeze*
Soot ... *they grow it by the foot*
Goats ... *eating all the oats*
Bees ... *with little knobby knees*
Owls ... *shredding paper towels*
Apes ... *eating all the grapes*
Turtles ... *wearing rubber girdles*
Bear ... *with curlers in its hair*
Buffaloes ... *with hair between their toes*
Foxes ... *stuffed in little boxes*
Coke ... *enough to make you choke*
Pepsi ... *that gives you apoplexy*
Flies ... *swarming round the pies*
Fishes ... *sitting in the dishes*
Moths ... *eating through the cloth*
Scouts ... *eating brussels sprouts*

*Jonah agreed to put the armour on only after the crew
promised that it would help him to float.*

SEA SAYINGS

Toe the line

One explanation of this everyday saying is that when a ship's crew
were ordered to 'fall in' they would line up on deck. To ensure a neat
alignment of each row, the sailors were directed to stand with their
toes just touching a particular seam between a pair of planks. Anyone
who disobeyed was told to 'toe the line'.

HERE BE MONSTERS!

Tales of strange sea creatures that attack boats and drag sailors to their deaths have been around for as long as men have gone to sea. A look back at ancient charts shows strange illustrations of sea monsters and giant fish – usually at the extremities of the charted areas. Few people believe in sea monsters these days, yet there are still many mysteries that lie beneath the sea.

Whales and some of the larger sharks probably gave rise to the first tales of sea monsters, and both have been known to attack ships and yachts, but it is the giant squid that keeps the sea monster myth alive today.

Scientifically known as *Architeutis dux*, it is the largest of all invertebrates and can reach 60 feet in length. Recent seafarers' accounts of encounters involve sightings of giant squid more than 130ft long. Round-the-world yachtsmen have reported squid of over 30ft attaching themselves to their boats but marine biologists have yet to observe a giant squid alive.

Exploration of the deepest, darkest depths is only just beginning, with remote submarines allowing cameras to discover new creatures that exist far beyond man's realm. Perhaps there be monsters after all.

TRAFFIC LIGHTS

Confined entrances to ports and harbours are sometimes controlled by a system of traffic lights, which are usually three vertical lights.

Three red flashing	Serious emergency – stop or divert
Three red	Do not proceed
Three green	Proceed, one-way traffic
Top two green	Proceed, two-way traffic
Top and bottom green	Proceed only when instructed

SAILING TERMS THAT CONFUSE LANDLUBBERS

Tack

A shop that is full of tack will contain a variety of novelty cruet sets, posters of cats in amusing poses and plastic fish that sing to you each time you walk past. A stable that is full of tack will have saddles, crops, stirrups and bridles hanging from every wall. You can even use a tack to hold down a carpet. But ignore all that. When sailing, to tack means to change course by passing the bow of the boat through the wind. Such a manoeuvre is consequently known as a tack. Simple – except that you have to remember that tack also refers to the lower forward corner of a sail.

CRUISING COCKTAILS

Harbour Lights

Always a welcome sight at the end of a long day on the water. Pour a couple of fingers of vodka into a glass, bailer or compass cover. Add four fingers of peach juice (in emergency use the syrup from one of those cans you've got stuck at the back of a locker). Top up with cranberry juice and a splash of lemonade.

WORDS ON THE WATER

Frank Cowper explains how yachtsmen coped without GPS at the turn of the nineteenth century. It had been calm most of the day, and I only passed the Udder Beacon in the gloaming. A haze spread over the sea at sunset, and Gribbin Head faded from sight before I could make out objects clearly. There was no light on St Catherine's Point then, and the leading light into Fowey was given as red, fixed. I knew I should have to go very close to the W shore before seeing anything of the entrance, so I held on in the darkness, listening keenly. I could see nothing except a dark undistinguishable mass on my right, but could hear the sea breaking on the rocks. The breeze was light off shore. When the noise of the sea became too acute ahead I went about, for I feared the Cannis Rock, and could not tell how far I was off. Standing on for a bit on the next tack, again the sea seemed very loud, so once more I went about. There was a lull for a few minutes. When again the noise became too obtrusive. I luffed and listened. The noise was all round it seemed. Then I saw a light – a very dim one, and it kept going out, obscured, as I thought, by the rigging of some vessel, for it was white and I took it to be a riding light.

All this time the sound of the sea was unpleasantly audible. I lay to and sounded. No bottom at ten fathoms. All this time I felt the tide was taking me in. Suddenly I head a sharp crash close on my port. It was a wave breaking over a sunken rock. I hastily let the jib and fore sheets draw and went about. The light still blinked, so I let it blink and crept in with cautious, short tacks. Then I saw a thin looming on my starboard. It was a vessel, a fishing boat, no hands onboard, moored stern and stern. That would do. There was no swell. I must be inside. So, going gently alongside, I made fast head and stern, and put all snug for the night. It was late and I took no further notice of the blinking light, concluding it was too thick to see the red light. Next morning I found I had done very well. I was off Polruan, at the S end, and in as good a berth as I could be.

Frank Cowper, *Sailing Tours, Part II: The Nore to The Scilly Isles*

THE MEANING OF ENDURANCE

One of the greatest acts of seamanship ever undertaken in the last 100 years was that of Sir Ernest Shackleton on board a small open boat called the James Caird. Shackleton had been bound for Antarctica on the ship Endurance when she was caught in the ice and crushed. He and his crew had to leave her, take the ship's small lifeboats and seek dry land on 9 April 1916. This they did, but were little better off as they were then marooned on Elephant Island, 800 miles south of Cape Horn, with little food and no chance of rescue. Shackleton ordered for the James Caird, a 23ft whaler, to be modified with a deck and extra ballast.

On 24 April he set sail with five companions bound for South Georgia, 500 miles away. It was winter in the Antarctic and conditions were appalling for the men, who did not have the benefit of modern clothing or navigation equipment. Shackleton and his crew survived constant storms, giant waves and icebergs and made landfall on South Georgia after 14 days at sea. However they were far from saved as they had landed on the uninhabited side of the island and faced a near-impossible crossing of the island's frozen, mountainous interior. Against all odds they made it.

The next morning Shackleton left on a whaler to rescue the men he had left on Elephant Island. However pack ice forced the ship back on that and two subsequent rescue attempts. It was fourth time lucky on 30 August 1916, when Shackleton's ship was sighted. Within hours the 23 men were safely returning to a world that had heard no news from them since October 1914; they had survived on Elephant Island for 105 days. Their extraordinary experiences would make them famous, and the leadership and seamanship of Shackleton would make him a hero.

TEN TYPES OF ICE

Anchor ice	Submerged ice attached or anchored to the bottom
Bare ice	Ice without snow cover
Brash ice	Accumulations of ice made up of fragments not more than 2m across
Compact ice	No water is visible
Fast ice	Sea ice that forms and remains fast along the coast
Firn	Old snow that is not as dense as ice
Floe	A flat piece of ice 20m of more across
Ice cake	A flat piece of ice less than 20m across
Nunatak	Rocky outcrop projecting from and surrounded by a glacier or ice sheet
Thaw holes	Vertical holes in sea ice

SCURVY

For 300 years, up to 1800, more seafarers died for want of a lemon than for any other reason. Scurvy, a disease caused by a deficiency of vitamin C (ascorbic acid), manifests itself as spongy, bleeding gums, hard patches on the skin, weakness and, ultimately, death. It is easily cured by a diet containing fresh fruit and vegetables and is unlikely to arise before six weeks of dietary neglect. Captain Cook ensured his men had a varied diet and thus kept scurvy at bay, but he had not realised the crucial role of vitamin C. In 1753 a scientist called James Lind published a treatise urging the Navy to issue lemon juice as a preventative. Forty years later they took his advice and scurvy was soon wiped out. It did, however, reappear a few decades later when limes were substituted for lemons. Their lower levels of ascorbic acid failed to prevent scurvy but did give Britons the reputation for being 'Limeys'.

NAUTICAL PUZZLES

Rearrange this observation to discover the first rule of sinking
Trim candid Helen frowns
Answer on page 153

CHANGING CHARTS

Charts change. This may be because a buoy has been placed over a new hazard, or because a sand bank has appeared where once there was deep water. Cartographers can make mistakes too – an alarming but unavoidable fact.

To ensure that he is carrying the most accurate chart, a sailor must check to see if any of the charts he carries have been updated. All hydrographic offices issue regular corrections, in the form of Notices to Mariners, for their paper and electronic charts. Private paper chartmakers do the same. The notices tell you what to cross out, add or move. If there are complicated changes to a small area then a 'patch' will be issued. This is a portion of the chart that can be cut out and stuck over the area of chart to be amended.

Up until five or six years ago, Notices to Mariners were issued in paper form on a weekly basis, with monthly and annual summaries. There was then an intermediate period in which most hydrographic offices also made them available on the internet. Over the past year one or two hydrographic offices (including the British Admiralty) have been steadily phasing out the paper version. Access to the internet is now essential to keep charts updated and shows how technology has become part of all sailors' lives, whether they like it or not.

Draught, in centimetres, of the Bénéteau Océanis 321 (shallow draught version)

Kite-surfing is the most extreme form of sailing and one of the fastest-growing sports in the world. Go down to almost any long, sandy beach and you are likely to see someone with a wet suit, a small surfboard and a large kite. The kite-surfer wears a harness to which the kite is attached and has two lines to control the kite: pull left and it goes left, right and it goes right. It may sound simple, but in practice it is another matter.

Keeping the huge expanse of canvas balanced in the air above you while you wade into the surf and attempt to get your feet into the straps of your board is very difficult – and you haven't even started the surfing bit yet. Next comes the moment of truth: by pulling on one of the strings, the kite swoops through the air, accelerating rapidly and generating huge lift. In an instant you are away, skimming over the water with one eye on the sea and the other on the kite – as soon as it stops moving you start to sink. To keep the kite powered up, the surfer must tug his strings so that it stays in the 'power zone' – go too far to one side or the other and it will stop pulling and eventually collapse.

If the kite ends up in the drink all is not lost. One edge is inflatable, and this is pumped up before it is launched. If the kite crashes, it will remain afloat and a couple of tugs of the line should have it soaring into the air again. When the kite-surfer has had his fun, he returns to the beach, packs his kite into a ruck-sack, tucks his board under his arm and throws the lot into the boot of his car.

The fact that the kites pull up as well as along allows skilled kite-surfers to perform incredible stunts, literally hanging in the air as they twist and turn. A professional circuit is now well-established and a range of disciplines allow all aspects of this thrilling sport to be showcased. There are also open water races with fleets of kite-surfers flitting across the water beneath the colourful canopies of their kites.

But not all sailors are thrilled by the popularity of kite-surfing. The sport attracts thrill seekers who may have little idea of the nautical rules of the road. Kite-surfers can easily exceed 20 knots as they flash across the water and some yachtsmen see them as hazard to everyone on the water, although they may just be jealous.

QUOTES ON BOATS

What bliss to be in the cockpit with the sun and the warm breeze on one's skin, just watching the sea, and the sky, and the sails.
Sir Francis Chichester, yachtsman

DO YOU WANT ICE WITH THAT?

For home waters sailors, ice is merely an innocent ingredient in the après sail G&T, but for those voyaging to the high latitudes, it poses a grave threat. Taking the temperature of the air of the water is not a reliable way to detect the proximity of an iceberg, nor is listening for an echo from a whistle or siren. More reliable indications that an iceberg is nearby include coming across an area of calm water in open sea, suggesting that an iceberg is to windward. A sound like gunfire may be the noise of part of an iceberg breaking off to create a growler. The sound of waves breaking on the shore when there is no nearby land is another chilling indication that an iceberg is nearby.

INTO THE DEPTHS

The traditional markings on a leadline

Two fathoms	Two strips of leather
Three fathoms	Three strips of leather
Five fathoms	A piece of white rag
Seven fathoms	A piece of red bunting
10 fathoms	A piece of leather with a hole in it
13 fathoms	A piece of blue serge
15 fathoms	Another piece of white rag
17 fathoms	Another piece of red bunting
20 fathoms	Two knots

Leadlines should be wetted and stretched prior to marking.
One fathom equals six feet, or 1.8288 metres.

I THINK I'LL BUILD MY BOAT WITH...

Wood

Wood certainly has its appeal as a boatbuilding material. Natural beauty comes high on most people's lists – there is something very special about wood that continues to live and breathe long after it has been felled. It may be roughly hewn and weather-beaten, or it might be immaculately varnished, but wood speaks to a sailor's soul as no other material can. The fact that wood floats, unlike most other materials used to build boats, probably makes it attractive at some subconscious level.

That's the romance; in practice it can be a different matter. Wood demands care and attention like no other material. It will look after you only if you look after it. That means plenty of painting and varnishing, tracking down leaks and tackling rot and worm. The wooden boats that are being built today tend to be very beautiful and very expensive.

A spot of trouble at the windward mark meant that sailing would not reappear as an Olympic sport for many years.

NAUTICAL PUZZLES

Rearrange this sentence to discover where this action takes place:
He eases vents
Answer on page 153

NOT THAT TOUR DE FRANCE

The French love their cycling and the Tour de France is the greatest cycling race in the world. They also love their sailing, a fact reflected by the interest the nation has in the Tour de France *à la Voile*.

The racing takes place among a fleet of identical Mumm 30 yachts, designed by Bruce Farr. The boats are fast and exciting yet relatively uncomplicated and economical, making them attractive to sponsors. The events are held at the same time as the cycle race and involves a series of races along the English Channel, the Atlantic Coast and the Mediterranean. There are inshore thrashes as well as coastal hops, allowing skippers and crews to show off their skills in a wide variety of conditions. Professional teams race for line honours in each event but the large fleet also includes a number of amateur and student crews.

WORDS ON THE WATER

The ship Columbia Rediva, Pacific Ocean, 1791
Between the hours of 3pm and 4pm, departed this life our dear friend Nancy the Goat having been the Captain's companion on a former voyage around the Globe but her spirited disposition for adventure led her to undertake a second voyage of Circumnavigation; but the various changes of Climate, and sudden transition from the Polar Colds to Torrid Zone, prov'd too much for a constitution naturally delicate. At 5pm committed her body to the deep. She was lamented by those who got a share of her milk!

John Boit in the log of the ship Columbia Rediva

KNOT ANOTHER BOAT NAME

Knot To Worry	Knot Tonight
Knot Yours	Knot Wise
Knot-A-Wake	Knot-on-Call
Knot Again	Knot a Care
Knot a Yacht	Knot Bored
Knot 4 Sail	Knot for Long
Knot Home	Knot Shore
Knot Me	Knot on Duty
Knot Bad	Knot So Fast
Knot Paid For	

DON'T WHERRY, BE HAPPY

All round the world different vessels have evolved to suit the local waters in which they sail and the work they have to do. The waterways of Norfolk once carried corn and coal as well as anything else that needed transporting between farms, towns and ports. The vessel that most often moved those goods was the Norfolk wherry. With a 35m hold, the wherry could carry great loads among the protected inland waters but could also venture out to sea to pick up cargo from ships moored well offshore. The wherry was an adaptation of the Viking longboat, but with a huge gaff rig. The ability of these boats to sail to windward was so exceptional that locals initially thought that witchcraft must be involved. The wherry ruled the waves of Norfolk in the latter half of the nineteenth century, but improved roads and reliable lorries meant her working days were numbered. Some went on to be used as hunting launches or houseboats, others were converted to become pleasure craft. But they are demanding craft to maintain and now just a handful are still afloat – although if you peer among the Norfolk rushes, you might well find a wherry waiting to be resurrected from the mud.

A NAUTICAL LIMERICK

There was a young sailor named Bates
Who danced the fandango on skates.
He fell on his cutlass
Which rendered him nutless
And practically useless on dates.

WATERSPOUTS

Waterspouts are perhaps the most spectacular meteorological phenomenon that can be witnessed at sea. They are essentially mini tornados and can occur anywhere that the water is noticeably warmer than the air and there are thunderclouds forming.

Cold air is warmed by the warmer water and starts to rise, and this process is exaggerated by the thundercloud above that sucks up the warm moist air. In these unstable conditions a bulge of cloud can emerge from the bottom of the thundercloud with powerful downdrafts of wind. These downdrafts are matched by the swirling of air upwards. These two actions result in a swirling effect and the bulge becomes a rotating trunk. The trunk sucks up warm air, which is full of energy, making it larger and more powerful. When the trunk reaches the water, more energy is added to the equation, with warm water being sucked upwards, intensifying the process even more. Winds inside a waterspout can reach 150 knots and while it is extremely rare for a yacht to be struck by one, the effects are normally devastating. If you see a waterspout forming while afloat, sail at right angles to the direction in which the clouds are travelling.

SEA SINGERS

Bands with a nautical sound

The Beach Boys
Bow Wow Wow
Creedence Clearwater Revival
Flock of Seagulls
Katrina and the Waves
The Lighthouse Family
Ocean Colour Scene
Sailor
The Seahorses
Starsailor
The Waterboys

Yachtsmen have a special relationship with the animals that live in the sea. There are many stories of single-handed yachtsmen who refuse to catch fish because they feel some strange bond with these creatures for whom the sea is also their whole world. Some fish will swim for thousands of miles in the shadow cast by a yacht's hull and there are sailors who develop a real fondness for these scaly companions. Other yachtsmen save their affections for fellow mammals with whom they share the sea.

Porpoises, dolphins and whales are naturally drawn to yachts, whether out of curiosity, playfulness or to establish that there is no risk from these strange intruders into their world. Dolphins are a particular delight and their playfulness is legendary. It is not uncommon for sailors to come across pods containing too many dolphins to count and a display of aquatic acrobatics is almost guaranteed. Then, as quickly as the dolphins come, they go again, leaving you in silent awe of their grace and speed.

Whales are even more impressive, though are seen less often. They are also feared by many sailors, and with good reason. Hitting a whale can be catastrophic for a small boat. The whale will probably escape with a headache, but the yacht is more likely to spring a leak that could sink it. Mid-ocean collisions are frighteningly common but happen so quickly that it is often impossible to determine whether the object that was struck really was a whale and not a log or some other piece of ocean debris.

Not that all whale encounters are accidental. Tales are told of whales attacking yachts and it is a worrying time for any skipper when he knows he is sailing through a pod of whales. These mighty mammals will often swim very close to boats before submerging. The wait is agonising – will the creature rise up beneath the keel and up-end the yacht, or leave it to sail on? Attacks are rare, though in the summer of 2003 a yacht chartered by an English family was attacked by a whale while sailing among the Whitsunday Islands, off Australia. The whale rose up from the water and crashed down on the yacht, smashing its rigging and knocking its mast down. It is thought that the yacht had sailed between a mother whale and her calf and she reacted as any mother would.

It is always a treat to sail with dolphins and whales and their unpredictability is just one of the things that makes encounters with these fascinating animals so thrilling.

110 *Length, in feet, of Team Adventure, the 60ft wide maxi-catamaran skippered by Cam Lewis*

GLAD TIDINGS

The oceans that cover the earth are subject to the gravitational pull of the moon and sun. These forces, coupled with the rotation of the Earth, give rise to the tides that cause the water level to rise and fall around our coasts. The coming and going of this water results in tidal streams and these can dramatically help or hinder a sailor trying to get from A to B. The direction and rates of tide are recorded in Tidal Atlases, which allow the sailor to see whether the movement of the water will be with or against him. If it's with, he may be in port an hour or two sooner, if against, he may not get there at all. Sailing against a foul tide (one that is running in the opposite direction to that in which you want to go) can be the equivalent of walking up the down escalator: plenty of movement but no progress.

Tides are often accelerated as they are pushed around headlands or between landmasses. Tides of around two knots are common around Britain's coast, although flows of 16 knots have been recorded off the coast of Scotland.

QUOTES ON BOATS

A collision at sea can ruin your entire day.
Thucydides, ancient Greek historian

BEST SCILLY BEACHES

The Isles of Scilly are a dream destination for many yachtsmen. Lying in the warming Gulf Stream current they boast a semi-tropical climate and in settled weather could easily be mistaken for a corner of the Caribbean. There are many anchorages, though none offers protection from all directions, making a trip to the Scillies something of a gamble. If you do sail there you will be able to explore the countless stunning beaches that fringe the islands. According to the islanders, the top 10 beaches are:

1. Great Bay on St Martin's
2. Pentle Bay on Tresco
3. Rushy Bay on Bryher
4. Pelistry Bay on St Mary's
5. The Bar on St Agnes
6. Bar Point on St Mary's
7. Lawrence's Beach on St Martin's
8. Landing Beach on Samson
9. Appletree Bay on Tresco
10. Great Porth on Bryher

In sea affairs, nothing is impossible.
Vice Admiral Lord Nelson, naval commander

WORDS ON THE WATER

Maurice and Maralyn Bailey were left with just a life raft and small dinghy then their yacht sank in the middle of the Pacific. After 117 days adrift their chances of survival were slim...

Someone was shaking me, a disembodied voice was calling, 'Maurice,' and again 'Maurice...' I thought, 'For pity's sake leave me alone.'

'Get out to the dinghy. A ship is coming,' Maralyn's urgent tone had penetrated my sluggish brain. Cursing, I automatically struggled to a kneeling position and scrambled across to the dinghy. I sat on the thwart in a dazed condition, trying to focus my eyes on to different parts of the sea. Maralyn was standing in the raft waving her jacket. Yet I could see no ship; Maralyn must be imagining things.

'Wave your jacket, it's there, behind you.'

'All right,' I said turning slowly. Then I saw it; a small white, rust streaked ship approaching from the east. It would pass very close and I began to wave my oilskin jacket. The ship steamed on a course nearly due west and within a short time it was opposite us, about half a mile away.

'It's a Korean fishing boat,' I called to Maralyn. 'Remember seeing them in Tenerife?'

Maralyn answered but did not stop waving. Her vigorous movements rocked the raft with its nearly deflated lower section almost under water. The ship went past and I stopped waving. It was no use, the ship was not going to stop. Why waste any more energy? I felt ill and slumped to my knees.

I called to Maralyn, 'Stop waving, save your strength.' She ignored me and continued to wave as the ship showed its stern to us. It was the first we had seen for 43 days.

'Please come back,' Maralyn shouted. 'Please...'

I was oblivious now of the ship's movements as I knelt in the dinghy. Maralyn was still imploring the ship to return. Let it go on, I thought, this is our world now, on the sea, amongst the birds and the turtles and the fish.

Maralyn had suddenly stopped her entreaties but continued to wave her jacket quietly. I looked up and stared for some time at the ship. I looked long and hard at in disbelief. Was it returning or was it a trick of my eyes? Maralyn looked across at me. 'It's coming back,' she said.

Maurice and Maralyn Bailey,
117 Days Adrift

THE REALITY OF SAILING

Toast

It may seem an incredibly petty moan but the fact that you can't get a good bit of toast at sea is something that can weigh heavily on a yachtsman's mind during a long cruise or ocean passage. Some yachts will have a socket into which a toaster can be plugged, but these will normally work only when one is in harbour and connected into power from the shore. Ovens can be bought that include grills, but these are rare and can be expensive. The average sailor is therefore left with making toast on his gas hob. As much thought and ingenuity has been put into how to do this successfully as has been devoted to the design of any other piece of yachting equipment. There are numerous contraptions that seek to diffuse the heat of the flame and turn bread from soft and white to crisp and golden brown, but none of them succeed. The result is almost always a burnt exterior while the inside of the bread is totally uncooked. There is, in addition, an inevitable taste of gas to the 'toast'. Some sailors throw their toasters overboard and buy crispbread instead. Others waft their slice of bread over the flame, like some Victorian pantry maid with a toasting fork. Using a dry non-stick saucepan is also alleged to work though is yet to catch on.

The simple truth is that if you want a perfect piece of toast you will have to stay at home.

OYSTER DREDGERS

Set sail on the River Fal on a chill autumn day and you will not be alone. The yachtsmen who sail for pleasure will probably be sitting snug in their marinas, leaving the waters of the Fal to the men who sail for a living. But these are not professional racers with six-figure salaries: they are Cornishmen dredging for oysters.

Local regulations prohibit the use of power-driven vessels with which to dredge for oysters and so the fishermen do it the old-fashioned way. With a scrap of sail hoisted, they make their way to windward, their nets scouring the riverbed for the oysters that will fetch a high price in the markets of London and beyond. Dredging by sail in a traditional working boat is less efficient than using a modern boat with an engine and powered winches, and so the oyster stocks are not depleted, meaning the industry can continue from one year to the next. It's a piece of practical ecological legislation that means hard work for the men who sail the boats, but creates a future for the industry and is a wonderful sight for anyone who sees these skilled sailors at work.

WHERE AM I?

The Global Positioning System (GPS) has changed the face of navigation forever. Just a few decades ago the idea of a small box no bigger than a mobile phone being able to provide your precise latitude and longitude seemed the stuff of science fiction. Today it is almost taken for granted.

GPS consists of 24 satellites circling the earth in six orbital planes at 55 degrees to the Equator. Three extra satellites are up there as active spares, waiting to take over if another satellite fails. The satellites beam down information, giving their own position at a given time. The delay between the information being transmitted and received on the ground is used to calculate the distance between the satellite and the receiver. With this information from three satellites, three intersecting range circles can be formed. The receiver is located where the circles cross.

The accuracy of GPS was artificially reduced until 2000 to prevent countries outside the West using it for military purposes. The Standard Positioning Service that is now available to yachtsmen is accurate to within about 20 metres, and current technological advances should improve accuracy to within two metres in the very near future.

NAUTICAL PUZZLES

Whose company is preferable during severe weather:
Taylor's or Graham's?
Answer on page 153

WORDS ON THE WATER

If a person suffer much from sea-sickness, let him weigh it heavily in the balance. I speak from experience: it is no trifling evil, cured in a week. If, on the other hand, he take pleasure in naval tactics, he will assuredly have full scope for his taste. But it must be borne in mind, how large a proportion of the time, during a long voyage, is spent on the water, as compared with the days in harbour. And what are the boasted glories of the illimitable ocean? A tedious waste, a desert of water, as the Arabian calls it. No doubt there are some delightful scenes. A moonlight night, with the clear heavens and the dark glittering sea, and the white sails filled by the soft air of a gently blowing trade-wind, a dead calm, with the heaving surface polished like a mirror, and all still except the occasional flapping of the canvas.

Charles Darwin, *The Voyage of the Beagle*

114 *Days it took the 262ft sailing ship British Merchant to make the passage from Liverpool to San Francisco, via Cape Horn*

SAILING STEREOTYPES

The dinghy dad

Walk the shore of any sailing club and you'll come across Dinghy Dad. He'll be on the foreshore with a pair of pliers, probably doing something illegal to the rig of his child's dinghy. Dinghy Dad can sail himself, but not particularly well. Having never made it to the Olympics or America's Cup, he is determined that his son or daughter will do so instead. The child is not always consulted about this mission but knows full well that failure on the water is not an option. Dinghy Dad will often take on responsibility for coaching whatever class his child sails in, allowing him to use the club rescue boat to pursue his offspring, shouting instructions and occasional threats. The high cost of the latest dinghy/sails/wetsuit is often used to blackmail the child into making greater efforts. If the child excels, the father will take the credit; if he fails, it will be due to youthful indolence and lack of application. No one likes a Dinghy Dad, least of all their poor child.

WHERE YACHTSMEN SHOULD LIVE

Hull
Keele
Rock
Sale
Winchester

THE PLIGHT OF THE ALBATROSS

The albatross occupies a special place in the heart of anyone who has spent time on the world's oceans. Sometimes these amazing birds will be your only companion for days, your only contact with the world beyond your vessel's hull.

And amazing they are. With its 12ft wingspan, an albatross can fly up to 1,615 miles in 24 hours, diving into waves to collect food ploughed up by the keels of ships. But now the albatross is falling victim to deep-sea fishing boats trailing 80-mile long lines covered with thousands upon thousands of hooks. Each hook is baited with squid to persuade valuable fish to bite and secure their fate as Japanese sushi. But more than 100,000 albatrosses fall victim to these lures a year. These fishing fleets operate beyond the law and have no concerns other than the price their catch will fetch. The fact that the albatross may join the dodo is of no interest to them, though international pressure may help stop deaths. To learn more, visit www.savethealbatross.org.

I NAME THIS SHIP

The US Navy has an unofficial tradition of naming certain types of ship after certain things...

Type of Craft	Named After
Aircraft carriers	battles, famous Americans
Ammunition ships	volcanoes, fire/explosion terms
Amphibious command ships	mountains, mountain ranges
Battleships	US states
Cargo ships	heavenly bodies, US counties
Cruisers	US cities
Destroyer tenders	US locations and areas
Destroyers	late Navy and Marine Corps heroes
Hospital ships	assistance-related mission terms
Minesweepers	danger-related terms
Nuclear submarines	famous Americans
Oilers	rivers, shipbuilders
Store ships	heavenly bodies
Submarine rescue vessels	birds
Older submarines	fish and sea creatures
Tugboats	Native American tribes and terms

QUOTES ON BOATS

*The charm of single-handed cruising is not
solitude, but independence.*
Claud Worth, yachtsman

SEASICKNESS

The dreaded *mal de mer* can strike even the hardiest yachtsman. Many of the great voyagers spent the first few days at sea with their head over the side, feeding the fish. Tracy Edwards, famed skipper of Maiden, the all-girl round the world yacht, is reputed to do little but feed the fish for 36 hours before she finds her sea legs.

Cures for seasickness are legion and while some of them work for some sailors some of the time, none work for all sailors all of the time. Ginger biscuits are meant to help, as is scanning the horizon or taking a turn at the helm. Drugs help some but send others to sleep. One patch that can be placed behind the ear has been known to cause hallucinations – just what you don't want in the middle of a night watch.

There is one thing that always works and the unafflicted take great joy in telling their stricken shipmate about it. The magic cure? To sit under a tree.

SEA SAYINGS

Wipe the slate clean

A slate tablet was kept near the helm on which the watch keeper would record the speeds, distances, headings and tacks during the watch. If the slate was wiped clean at the start of a new watch all previous incidents could be forgotten.

HOW TO FIRE A CANNON

Should you ever find yourself required to fire a cannon, these orders – as issued by a captain in Nelson's navy – to fire and reload a loaded stowed cannon might come in handy:

Silence!
Cast loose your gun!
Level your gun!
Take out your tampion!
Prime!
Run out your gun!
Fire!
Worm and sponge!
Load with cartridge!
Load with shot and wad your shot!
Ram home shot and wad!
Put in your tampion!
House your gun!
Secure your gun!

FLASH – AAH!

You can see many spectacular natural phenomena at sea. Waterspouts and whirlpools are impressive but the rarest and most magical sight of all is the green flash at sunset.

If conditions are just right, a bright flash appears along the horizon just as the sun is sinking beyond view. Those who have witnessed it say that it is incomparable.

The green flash happens so rarely that it has taken on a mythological status among seafarers, but there is a perfectly good explanation for the marine pyrotechnics.

The flash is caused by refractive separation of the sun's rays into its spectral components. The curvature of the Earth means that as the sun sets it shines through the sea with the water acting as a filter – when refractive conditions are suitable, red, orange and yellow waves of sunlight are not refracted sufficiently to reach the eye, whereas green waves are. The visual result is a green flash in the surrounding sky.

'And I say this would have never happened if we'd bought a caravan instead of this bloody boat.'

ULYSSES THE CAR FERRY

Keep an eye out for Ulysses if you're sailing up the Irish Sea – not the mythical adventurer but the biggest car ferry in the world. With a cargo of 2,000 people and 1,000 cars and trucks, Ulysses plies her trade between Dublin and Holyhead, North Wales. Claiming to hold more vehicles than Dublin's five biggest car parks, the £300 million Ulysses is certainly an impressive sight as she towers above the stormy seas between Britain and Ireland. Her enormous four-bladed propellers drive her through gales that keep smaller ferries in port, while the thrusters that are used to help her dock have a combined power of 12,000hp – more than some ferries have in their main engines. In 10-metre seas, Ulysses can still make over 20 knots, ensuring that she keeps to her timetable and that she is trusted by haulage companies and holidaymakers alike. Giant stabilising fins help her cope with the swell of the Irish Sea and make sure that those on board can walk among the bars, restaurants, shops and casino without lurching about.

THE MYSTERY OF THE MARY CELESTE

There are many myths and strange tales associated with the sea, but the one that has best stood the test of time is the mystery of the Mary Celeste.

Built in 1860, Mary Celeste was 103ft long and a capable ocean-going sailing vessel. On 7 November 1872, she set off from New York. On board was Captain Briggs, his wife and young daughter, and a crew of eight. The hold was full of 1,700 barrels of raw American alcohol, bound for Genoa.

On 4 December the Mary Celeste was sighted by another vessel. As it drew near, it became apparent that there was no one on board. The Mary Celeste was utterly deserted. Her logbook had been filled in up to 24 November – but that was 10 days earlier and her recorded position was more than 400 miles from where she was found. Could this ghost ship have sailed so far by herself? It seemed impossible. Her sails were properly set on the starboard side. However, going by the record in her logbook, the sails should have been set to port. The changing direction of the wind meant that someone, or something, must have been onboard to tack her and reset the sails, and within the last few days. But who? Or what?

And what of the captain, his family and the crew? Accounts vary, not helped by a lurid retelling of the story by Arthur Conan Doyle. Some say that there was no evidence of violence or foul play, others describe blood-smattered sails and cutlasses lying on deck. Some say that the ship's rowing boat was missing – could the crew have murdered Briggs and escaped? Surely not – it would have been near suicide to cast off in a small boat in the mid-Atlantic.

Was foul weather, not foul play responsible? Could a giant wave have swept all 11 people overboard? Unlikely. What if pirates had attacked? But then why was the valuable cargo untouched. So many questions, so few credible answers.

The story of the Mary Celeste has proved irresistible for more than 100 years. The ghost ship of the Atlantic is used to prove or disprove the latest weird and wonderful theory. Sea monsters, sea quakes, alien abduction – they all have their adherents and the more people who investigate the fate of the Mary Celeste, the more mysterious the story becomes.

QUOTES ON BOATS

We may have all come on different ships,
but we're in the same boat now.
Martin Luther King Jr, civil rights campaigner

Number of days (after handicap adjustment) it took Cornelis van Rietschoten, 119
on the 65ft ketch Flyer, to win the 1977 Whitbread Round the World Race

SAILING TERMS THAT CONFUSE
LANDLUBBERS

Spar

To some this is a convenient local store selling overpriced toilet paper, to others it is a boxing workout, and to the hard of spelling it is a health resort. However, at sea a spar is none of these. For 'spar', read 'big stick', as spars are the masts, booms and other big sticks from which the sails are hoisted and held aloft. Originally all spars were the trunks and branches of trees, but hollow metal masts were found to be lighter and now high-tech carbon spars are de rigueur on extreme racing yachts. This may help a yacht sail faster, but broken masts can no longer be replaced by stolen telegraph poles, as they could in the good old days.

WALLS OF WATER

Waves pose a far greater threat to the safety of sailors than does the wind. A well-found (well-built, solid) vessel with enough sea room can ride out high winds as long as the seas do not become too rough. But freak waves can strike ships almost out of the blue.

Rogue waves emerge from relatively calm seas with no storms for hundreds of miles. Trains of swells travelling in the same direction but at different speeds will pass through one another; when their crests, troughs and lengths happen to coincide they reinforce each other, combining their energies to form unusually large waves that tower mountainously for a few minutes then subside. Such giants can suddenly reach several times the height of most of the waves around them, forming mid-ocean breakers that are probably responsible for at least some mysterious disappearances of ships.

REASONS TO GO TO NEWLYN

Few yachtsmen venture beyond the granite mass of Cornwall's Lizard peninsula to the ports of Penzance and Newlyn. The wreck-strewn coastland puts many sailors off, although those who do go the extra mile are rewarded. Not only does Newlyn boast one of the country's busiest fish markets, it also hosts a unique tidal observatory.

The observatory is located at the end of the harbour's south pier and was established to determine the mean sea level that is used to calculate sea-level measurements across the UK. The mean sea level by which all others are measured was determined between 1915 and 1921 when the height of the water was noted every 15 minutes, 24 hours a day, every day of the year. From these observations the mean sea level was established and is marked by a brass bolt set into the ground.

The next wave rolled over the spot, and the next, but the boat did not reappear. The Alma rushed by the place. A little riffraff of oats and boxes was seen. An arm thrust up and a shaggy head broke surface a score of yards away.

For a time there was silence. As the end of the lake came in sight, the waves began to leap aboard with such steady recurrence that the correspondents no longer chopped ice but flung the water out with buckets. Even this would not do, and, after a shouted conference with Rasmunsen, they attacked the baggage. Flour, bacon, beans, blankets, cooking-stove, ropes, odds and ends, everything they could get hands on, flew overboard. The boat acknowledged it at once, taking less water and rising more buoyantly.

'That'll do!' Rasmunsen called sternly, as they applied themselves to the top layer of eggs.

'The h-hell it will!' answered the shivering one, savagely. With the exception of their notes, films, and cameras, they had sacrificed their outfit. He bent over, laid hold of an egg-box, and began to worry it out from under the lashing.

'Drop it! Drop it, I say!'

Rasmunsen had managed to draw his revolver, and with the crook of his arm over the sweep head, was taking aim. The correspondent stood up on the thwart, balancing back and forth, his face twisted with menace and speechless anger.

'My God!'

So cried his brother correspondent, hurling himself, face downward, into the bottom of the boat. The Alma, under the divided attention of Rasmunsen, had been caught by a great mass of water and whirled around. The after leach hollowed, the sail emptied and jibed, and the boom, sweeping with terrific force across the boat, carried the angry correspondent overboard with a broken back. Mast and sail had gone over the side as well. A drenching sea followed, as the boat lost headway, and Rasmunsen sprang to the bailing bucket.

Jack London,
The One Thousand Dozen

TYPES OF ROPE

Type of rope	Key properties
Polypropylene	Cheap, light, floats
Nylon	Strong and stretchy
Polyester	Strong, low stretch
High Modulus Polyethylene	Strong, light low stretch
Vectran	Very strong, very low stretch
PBO	Exceptionally strong, very low stretch, very expensive

WHAT'S IN A NAME

Celebs who sound as if they should be at sea...
Brian Ferry
Rod Hull
Roger Moore
Billy Ocean
Diana Rigg
David Seaman
Sandy Shaw
Howard Stern
Pete Waterman

THE ROUND THE ISLAND RACE

Every summer the waters of the Solent are virtually obscured for one day by the hundreds of yachts that compete in a race around the Isle of Wight. First sailed in 1931, the competitors in the Round the Island Race still compete for the Gold Roman Bowl, the legendary trophy presented by the race's founder Cyril Windeler. Little did he realise what he was starting. Today, there are often over 1,500 yachts, from maxi-yachts to the smallest offshore categories, and from speedy multihulls to sedate old-timers. With Admirals Cuppers competing alongside families having fun, the race is a multitude of races within a race. The start line is nautical chaos as the weekend cruisers get in the way of the hardcore racers and nimble sports boats flying past. Once past the rocks and wrecks of the Needles, things calm down a little, though if the tide is not kind and the wind is not strong, the stragglers may find themselves still at sea while the fastest crews are snug in the beer tent.

OLYMPIC SAILING BOATS AND CLASSES

Equipment	Event
Europe	Women's Single-handed Dinghy
Finn	Men's Single-handed Dinghy
470 Men	Men's Double-handed Dinghy
470 Women	Women's Double-handed Dinghy
49er	Open Double-handed High Performance Dinghy
Laser	Open Single-handed Dinghy
Mistral Men	Men's Windsurfer
Mistral Women	Women's Windsurfer
Star	Men's Double-handed Keelboat
Tornado	Open Double-handed Multihull
Yngling	Women's Triple-handed Keelboat

THE REALITY OF SAILING

Anchoring

There is a feeling among the sailing community that too many yachtsmen go from marina to marina, never stopping for the night at one of the countless anchorages around Britain's coast. Look closer and it becomes clear why this is so. On arrival at an anchorage there are bound to be a few yachts there before you. Each will have a skipper who will be keeping a keen eye on your movements in case you do anything to endanger his vessel. He'll shout the second that you start to drop the hook in the wrong place, but is unlikely to stand on the fore deck and cheerfully point out where his anchor is actually lying so that you can make a properly informed decision about where to drop your own. In the absence of such knowledge you'll just have to guess and hope all is well.

If the anchor holds then it'll be time to put the kettle on and wait for the next yacht to turn up so that you can watch them go through the same process. If you're not sure of your holding then you must hoist the hook and start all over again.

Perhaps you want to go ashore? Out with the dinghy and the pump and the oars and maybe the outboard too. But what if the wind shifts or someone fouls your anchor and sets you adrift? Best to play safe and stay put. Supper can be eaten in the cockpit, until the rain starts and you have to go below. But careful with the lights – you don't want to run the battery flat. And so to bed and blissful sleep – but what was that noise? Has the wind started to freshen already? Are you swinging? Has your transit shifted. No? Fine, back to half-sleep until the next grumble of anchor-chain over rock. Dawn comes and you set sail for the nearest marina and a bit of relaxation and a good night's sleep.

EARTHQUAKE!

You might think that an earthquake is the one hazard you wouldn't face at sea – but you'd be wrong. Severe quakes can cause tidal waves or shift the seabed so dramatically that you can be afloat one minute and aground the next. The Hydrographic Department of the Ministry of Defence has records of the damage caused by an earthquake off the coast of Portugal in 1969. The crew on one ship 100 miles away felt violent vibrations for about a minute. Another vessel the same distance away experienced a severe vertical shock. Meanwhile a motor tanker just 15 miles from the epicentre was lifted upwards and slammed down with such heavy vibrations that she was subsequently condemned as a total loss.

ROW, ROW, ROW YOUR BOAT

Simon Chalk was the first Briton to row solo across the Indian Ocean. His 3,010-mile, 107-day crossing in 2003 set a speed record and was the first to be officially recorded. Simon completed his task when he crossed the line of longitude north of Mauritius 108 days after he set off from Australia. Here's what he took on board:

2 Iridium satellite phones
2 video camcorders
1 handheld GPS
1 compass
1 water maker
2 fixed EPIRBs safety beacons
1 handheld EPIRB safety beacon
1 Argos tracking beacon
1 MP3 music juke box
1 fixed VHF radio
1 handheld VHF radio
3 dry cell batteries (power provided by solar)
Charts
1 fixed compass
60 days of full rations, contents as follows: three ready meals plus one pudding; three chocolate bars, one pack of biscuits, oatcakes, wine gums, chewing gum, one Pepperami.
100 days of drinks, contents as follows: four tea, two coffee, one hot chocolate, two energy powder sachets, plus numerous packs of sugar.
40 days of reduced rations, contents as follows: three dehydrated meals, two chocolate bars, one Pepperami, one pack of wine gums, one cereal bar.
Gas for cooking and 94 canisters (small)
5 gas stoves (4 spares)
2 strikers
100 waterproof matches
2 saucepans
2 Thermos flasks

3 Thermos mugs
6 plastic spoons

Safety: other
1 offshore distress flare kit
1 four-man life raft
2 life jackets
2 life lines
1 grab bag, contents: one litre of water, signalling mirror, six bars of chocolate, two rocket flares, one knife, first aid kit, survival blankets, one torch, one emergency fishing kit.
2 waterproof torches
1 survival knife
1 small drogue
1 para anchor

Rowing
3 sets of oars
3 rowing seats
2 spare rowing gates
4 sheeps' wool covers for seats
4 lots of seat padding foam
6 water bottles

Health
Suntan lotion
Sudacreem
After sun
Lip balm
Wet wipes
Comprehensive first aid kit
Vaseline
Toothpaste
Toothbrushes
Sun block
Clothing

Gerald had started to act differently since being made commodore of the yacht club.

WORDS ON THE WATER

From the ship's log of the brig Lucy, North Atlantic Ocean, southeast of New York, 19 September 1828.
Twelve at night double reefed the topsails, it blowing a dreadful gale. 4am split the foresail and fore topmast staysail. Then lay to under bare poles until 8 o'clock, put the helm up to windward to get the brig before the wind and found she would not fall off – put it alee and put all hands to throwing off the deck load, the sea making a complete breach over us. The gale still increasing Capt Church thought it best to cut away the mainmast, at 10am shipped a sea that took off both boats, water casks, quarter rails, and a large quantity of lumber, rigging, etc. The same sea washed Capt Church from the vessel and he was never seen afterwards.

WARM AND DRY

A generation of sailors is emerging that does not know what it is like to be really wet and cold. Their ignorance of these twin miseries is a result of the massive improvements made to sailing clothing. Whatever sort of boat you sail, and wherever you sail her, you will be warmer and drier than yachtsmen of yesteryear ever thought possible.

If you are more than 30 years old, you are likely to recall your dinghy sailing days: Peter Storm oilskins that crackled as you walked worn over a pair of jeans and a big jumper, plimsolls on your feet and a massive orange Crewsaver lifejacket on top of it all. Today's dinghy sailor will wear a wet suit, or even a dry suit, with neoprene boots and a slim buoyancy aid.

When they graduate to yachts, today's sailor will experience the joys of the layering system: a snug base layer, a fleece-lined mid layer and a totally waterproof top layer. All of it will be breathable to let the sweat out without letting the sea in. His boots will be breathable too and he will laugh at the thought of the yachtsman of old in his plastic boots and yellow sou'wester.

SEA SAYINGS

I don't like the cut of his jib

In days gone by, warships often had foresails (or jibs) shaped so that they could sail close to the wind and thus catch vessels to windward of them. Upon sighting these easily recognised foresails on a distant ship, a captain might declare that he did not like the cut of the other fellow's jib and attempt to flee.

HELICOPTER AHOY

On large vessels the following equipment should be to hand if a helicopter is about to land, to drop off or pick up people or goods.

Portable fire extinguisher
Large axe
Crowbar
Wire cutters
Static discharge/earthing pole
Red emergency signal/torch
Marshalling batons (at night)
First aid equipment

This equipment is not necessary on a yacht, but you must follow the helicopter pilot's instructions precisely and never attach any lines from the helicopter to the boat.

HOW TO GET KNOTTED

The reef knot

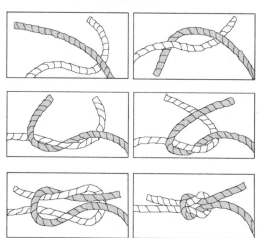

Take the left working end and cross it over and under the right working end.

Now tuck the new right working end over and under the new working end on the left. Pull on the both working ends to tighten.

Alternatively: left over right, under and through; right over left, under and through.

A YEAR IN THE LIFE OF THE RNLI

Crew member hours at sea: **53,732**

Services to merchant/fishing vessels: **948** *(11.7% of total services)*

Services to pleasure craft: **4,209** *(51.9% of total services)*

Services to people: **2,215** *(27.3% of total services)*

Services carried out in darkness **2,987** *(36.8% of total services)*

Services carried out in winds of Force Seven plus: **157** *(1.9% of total services)*

Days it took Yves Parlier to sail non-stop around the world to win the 2000 **127** *Vendée Globe Race*

QUOTES ON BOATS

There is no better company anywhere than men who love the sea.
John le Carré, novelist

KEEPING YOUR WOOD DRY

If a wooden boat absorbs water it will eventually rot. Various methods are used to prevent moisture absorption, though some are more effective than others.

Coating	Efficiency after 28 days (%)
Enamel	58
Oil paint	50
Lead paint	45
Varnish	20
Pink primer	14
Wax polish	3
Boiled oil and turps	>2
Raw linseed oil	>2

NAUTICAL PUZZLES

Which vice admiral might you find 50% of in a square ring?
Answer on page 153

WHAT A LOAD OF JUNK

Boats can hoist all sorts of sails in all sorts of arrangements but of all the options, the junk rig can claim to be one of the most long-lived. Thought of as quintessentially Chinese, the junk rig first appeared in Roman times, though it was not until 1959 that the cruising yachtsman started to consider it as an alternative to the modern Bermuda rig or more traditional gaff rig. The man who brought the junk rig to public attention was Blondie Haslar, who added an adapted 'Chinese rig' to his converted Folkboat. It was a strange combination but a successful one. Haslar came second in the first ever single-handed transatlantic race in 1960 and proved that the junk rig was a seaworthy set-up ideal for single-handers. There are fans of the junk rig around the country who proclaim its great downwind performance, ease of handling, simplicity and reliability. The sceptics point to the fact that junk rigs cope poorly in light winds and are less efficient to windward than conventional rigs with a mainsail and foresail. Both sides normally agree to disagree and one gets the feeling that the junk rig fans actually rather like being a bit different.

128 *Tins of shrimps consumed by Clare Francis and crew during their circumnavigation in the 1977–78 Whitbread Race*

I THINK I'LL BUILD MY BOAT WITH...

Aluminium

Most people compare aluminium to steel, the other raw material of choice if building a metal boat. It's certainly more expensive – 10 times or more – and is only about 65% as strong. So why use it? The reason is weight. It's only one third as heavy and that means an aluminium boat will be much faster than her steel sister.

It may not be pretty but aluminium can be left bare, unlike most other materials, and requires the minimum of maintenance. It won't rust but is highly vulnerable to electrolysis and to corrosion when in contact with other metals. Aluminium is stronger than other 'traditional' materials, meaning that you may be able to escape from a severe grounding that would have sunk a wooden or GRP boat.

WORDS ON THE WATER

Chale and Blackgang were there, dark and foreboding; the whole bay is a cruel lee-shore when

> *Leaps ashore the full sou'west*
> *All heavy-winged with brine*

'Keep her off-shore!' I called to my shipmate, now at the helm; 'Give the point a berth.'

He was gripping the tiller which kicked heavily now and again. He shoved it over with both hands turning her more off-shore.

The race off St Catherine's is rather an unaccountable affair, being sometimes tame and sometime very mutinous. It is of much less account than that of St Alban's, but if longer duration; it lasts all the way from St Catherine's to Dunnose, near Shanklin. The race would be in friendly mood to-day, though it would become more troublesome when the tide turned. And it *can* be quite nasty when it likes. We had hauled the Point abeam and the coast was changing every instant; Bonchurch Down was there, sloping toward the abrupt fall of Dunnose. A new reach of coast had taken the place of St Catherine's. And there, beyond Dunnose, was the gracious white line of Culver, on the horizon.

'This race is a paltry affair to-day,' I said; 'let's stand inshore and look at the country; there's lots of water.'

So with heed, for the wind was now almost dead aft and we ran the risk of a gybe, we shaped course closer inshore, scanning the broken dark cliffs with their ragged belt of wood below that velvet smoothness of the down. The landfall was stern, but it was noble. Growler rose and fell over the small, breaking hills of the sea, and swept rapidly on.

H Alker Tripp, *The Solent and the Southern Waters*

SONGS FOR SAILORS

Anchorage, Michelle Shocked
Dignity (A Ship Called), Deacon Blue
Driftwood, Travis
Ferry Cross the Mersey, Gerry and the Pacemakers
Fisherman's Dream, John Martyn
Fisherman's Song, Carly Simon
Friggin' in the Riggin', Sex Pistols
Love Boat, Kylie Minogue
Mermaids, Paul Weller
Queen of the Slipstream, Van Morrison
River Man, Nick Drake
Rudderless, Lemonheads
Sail Away, David Gray
Sail On, Commodores
Sailing, Rod Stewart
Sailor, Petula Clarke
Sailor to a Siren, Meat Loaf
Sailors Are Made to Travel, Edith Piaf
Seasick, Yet Still Docked, Morrissey
Ship to Shore, Chris de Burgh
Six Months in a Leaky Boat, Split Enz
The Tide is High, Blondie
Waves of Fear, Lou Reed

THE CINQUE PORTS

The Cinque Ports, on the coast of England, are so called because there were originally five of them, although there are now more. There is some debate about their origin, though it is most likely that the ports first came together informally during the eleventh century to regulate the important herring fair held each year at Yarmouth, on the Norfolk coast. From the twelfth century until the seventeenth century, these Kent and Sussex seaports were awarded special privileges in return for supplying ships and men for the defence of the Channel.

The original Cinque ports of Sandwich, Dover, Hythe, Romney and Hastings were joined in the thirteenth century by Rye and Winchelsea and in the next century gained full legal status as Ancient Towns. A large number of other towns became allied to the major ports and the 'coastal confederation' reached a total of 42 towns at its medieval peak – including many inland settlements.

The title of Lord Warden of the Cinque Ports has been held by, among others, the Duke of Wellington and Sir Winston Churchill.

BUOY OH BUOY!

It would seem common sense for navigation buoys to follow a standardised system so that wherever you sail you'd know whether, for example, you should pass to starboard or to port of a green buoy as you enter a harbour.

The marine rule makers tried to come up with such a system but failed. Their interesting compromise has been to agree a system in which the same buoys mean totally contradictory things depending on where in the world you are.

In the 1970s the International Association of Lighthouse Authorities (IALA) came up with an agreement about five types of buoy – lateral, cardinal, isolated danger, safe water and special – with specific rules for each. Of the five types, the most common are those using the lateral system. The madness came when lighthouse authorities were allowed the choice of using red to mean 'go to the left of me' or 'go the right of me' on a regional basis. It's like a red traffic light meaning 'go' in one part of the world and 'stop' in another.

So it is that in Europe, Asia, Africa and Australasia a green buoy tells the sailor to do one thing and in the Americas and the Caribbean it tells them to do the opposite.

NAUTICAL PUZZLES

Why did the water turn yellow?
Answer on page 153

SAILING STEREOTYPES

The old-time cruiser

The traditional cruiser does not hold with new-fangled inventions – like the internal combustion engine and electricity. No, things on his boat are simple and seaworthy. Well, simple at least. Our bearded friend (a beard is compulsory) will always drop anchor rather than pick up a buoy, even if he does so in the middle of a shipping lane. If he has to pick up a mooring he will, but he would rather be keel-hauled than tie up in a marina.

As well as a beard he always wears a battered hat with a small peak and a thick woollen jumper. The jumper stays on whatever the weather and there is no point telling him that a modern fleece is warmer, lighter, quicker-drying and cheaper. If it's new, the old-timer doesn't like it. He is almost always a single-hander, preferring the company of a good pipe and a trusted penknife.

It was only when construction was finished that they realised why the docks in Rugby were so much cheaper than those by the sea.

A NAUTICAL JOKE

A young wife, her boorish husband and a young good-looking sailor were shipwrecked on an island.

One morning, the sailor climbed a tall coconut tree and yelled, 'Stop making love down there!'

'What's the matter with you?' the husband said when the sailor climbed down. 'We weren't making love.'

'Sorry,' said the sailor, 'From up there it looked like you were.'

Every morning thereafter, the sailor scaled the same tree and yelled the same thing. Finally the husband decided to climb the tree and see for himself.

With great difficulty, he made his way to the top. When he looked down, the husband said to himself, 'By golly he's right! It does look like they're making love down there!'

WHISKY, HOTEL, ALFA, TANGO?

Radio reception at sea can often be unclear, with yachts pitching on the waves and motor boats not having the advantage of a mast on which to put their aerial. Add the sound of the wind and engines, and it can become necessary to spell important words phonetically. There is an agreed vocabulary to prevent misunderstandings, as follows:

Letter to be transmitted	Word to be used
A	Alfa
B	Bravo
C	Charlie
D	Delta
E	Echo
F	Foxtrot
G	Golf
H	Hotel
I	India
J	Juliet
K	Kilo
L	Lima
M	Mike
N	November
O	Oscar
P	Papa
Q	Quebec
R	Romeo
S	Sierra
T	Tango
U	Uniform
V	Victor
W	Whisky
X	X-ray
Y	Yankee
Z	Zulu

WORDS ON THE WATER

There be three things which are too wonderful for me. Yea four which I know not: the way of an eagle in the air; the way of a serpent upon a rock; the way of a ship in the midst of the sea; and the way of a man with a maid.

The Proverbs of Solomon, XXX, 18–19

PIRATES OF THE RED SEA

Piracy may not offer the career prospects that it did in the time of Sir Francis Drake, but it is still flourishing in a few corners of the world. Ships in some of the more remote parts of the Philippines are still likely to be attacked, and high seas highwaymen still operate among the myriad islands of northern Indonesia.

If you're after pirates closer to home, the Red Sea is your best bet, although the rumours exceed the risks. The pilot book to the region states that there were 15 recorded incidents between 1998 and 2001. Most of these took place near the coasts of Somalia and Yemen, and involved small, fast boats and heavily armed men. In all cases warning shots were fired.

If you are thinking of sailing through the Red Sea the advice is to:

- Sail in company
- Keep radio contact to a minimum
- Restrict use of lights at night
- If you are boarded, keep smiling
- Have some valuables hidden but ready to be discovered and surrendered
- Do not use firearms

ENSIGN ETIQUETTE

The ensign is the flag flown over the stern of a ship of yacht and is normally the national flag. The British red ensign contains the Union Flag in the top left corner of a red background and can be flown by all British yachts, registered or not. Under the Merchant Shipping Act all registered vessels are obliged to fly their ensigns when meeting other vessels, when entering or leaving foreign ports, or when approaching forts, signal and coastguard stations.

Members of the Royal Yacht Squadron may fly the white ensign while other selected organisations may fly the blue ensign or a defaced blue or red ensign.

It is considered good manners to fly your ensign in port during the official hours of daylight – these change around the world depending on the season. If an owner was giving up effective control of the vessel in the course of the day but people were remaining on board, it was deemed proper for the red and not a special ensign to be hoisted in the morning. The reason for this, given in the *Yachting World Handbook* of 1967, was that it was: 'considered demeaning to the status of ensigns to make exchanges of them during daylight'. Few people observe such niceties these days.

ALONE AROUND THE WORLD
IN AN OPEN BOAT

One of the greatest seafaring achievements, and one that went largely unnoticed, was the circumnavigation by a South African named Anthony Steward. Sailing around the world was nothing new, but what was remarkable is that he did it in an open boat.

NCS Challenger was 5.8m (19ft) long and had no cabin. There were waterproof lockers for clothes and food, but nowhere for Steward to escape the sun, wind and rain.

NCS Challenger had an open transom, meaning that the waves, which constantly broke over her, could drain freely off the back of the boat.

Capsizes were a routine occurrence for Steward, who was almost killed when his boat was struck by a cargo ship off South America. He was also dismasted in the Pacific and shipwrecked for nine days in a remote corner of the Seychelles. His voyage around the world took 260 days.

QUOTES ON BOATS

à donf (go for it)
Ellen MacArthur, yachtswoman

WORDS ON THE WATER

The first editor of Yachting Monthly *offers words of encouragement and caution nearly 100 years ago.*

Either of necessity or choice cruising is the form of sport adopted by the great majority of yachtsmen. While admitting that racing is the acme of pleasure to the sailor who knows, and can handle, his yacht, it must not be forgotten that cruising has a charm and a fascination which are too little known. We will make it our duty to give to the cruiser more attention than he has hitherto received, and in so doing we ask for his active cooperation.

Month by month we shall be glad to receive and buy for publication the best logs and cruising stories offered to us from all parts of the world. In this way we hope to put practical experience before our readers and admit many to the pleasures of the few. It is not sufficient, however, that a diarist has travelled far or that he has done so with great success. If he cannot clearly convey his experience and feelings, his work must be wasted as far as we are concerned. We want the actual experience of our writers, but we require them to be transmittable to others.

The Yachting Monthly No 1, Vol 1, May 1906

BEAUFORT WIND SCALE

Francis Beaufort was born in 1774 in County Meath, Ireland and began his nautical career aged 13 as a cabin boy in the Navy. He served in the Navy for 68 years, rising to the rank of Rear Admiral. He invented his famous wind scale in 1806 and it was adopted by the Royal Navy in 1838. It has changed little since.

Force	Wind (Knots)	Description	Effects on the Water	Effects on Land
0	< 1	Calm	Sea surface smooth and mirror-like	Calm, smoke rises vertically
1	1-3	Light Air	Scaly ripples, no foam crests	Smoke drift indicates wind direction, still wind vanes
2	4-6	Light Breeze	Small wavelets, crests glassy, no breaking	Wind felt on face, leaves rustle, vanes begin to move
3	7-10	Gentle Breeze	Large wavelets, crests begin to break, scattered whitecaps	Leaves and small twigs constantly moving, light flags extended
4	11-16	Moderate Breeze	Small waves, 1-4ft, becoming longer, numerous whitecaps	Dust, leaves, and loose paper lifted, small tree branches move
5	17-21	Fresh Breeze	Moderate waves, 4-8ft, taking longer form, many whitecaps, some spray	Small trees in leaf begin to sway
6	22-27	Strong Breeze	Larger waves, 8-13ft, whitecaps common, more spray	Larger tree branches moving, whistling in wires
7	28-33	Near Gale	Sea heaps up, waves 13-20ft, white foam streaks off breakers	Whole trees moving, resistance felt walking against wind

Force	Wind (Knots)	Description	Effects on the Water	Effects on Land
8	34-40	Gale	Moderately high (13-20ft) waves of greater length, edges of crests begin to break into spindrift, foam blown in streaks	Whole trees in motion, resistance felt walking against wind
9	41-47	Strong Gale	High waves (20ft), sea begins to roll, dense streaks of foam, spray may reduce visibility	Slight structural damage occurs, slate blows off roofs
10	48-55	Storm	Very high waves (20-30ft) with overhanging crests, sea white with densely blown foam, heavy rolling, lowered visibility	Seldom experienced on land, trees broken or uprooted, 'considerable structural damage'
11	56-63	Violent Storm	Exceptionally high (30-45ft) waves, foam patches cover sea, visibility more reduced	
12	64+	Hurricane	Air filled with foam, waves over 45ft, sea completely white with driving spray, visibility greatly reduced	[no land indication as trees and buildings have already been flattened]

SEA SAYINGS

No room to swing a cat

Not the literal meaning that many people imagine. On naval ships the
entire ship's company was required to witness flogging at close hand.
The crew would crowd around, meaning that the Bosun's Mate often
barely had enough room to swing his cat o' nine tails whip.

Beam, in centimetres, of a classic Canadian Westcoast sailing tender 137

THE LITTLE SHIP CLUB

When Mr R Gibbon wrote to *Yacht Sales and Charter* magazine in 1926 under the pen name of 'Keen but Ignorant', he could not have hoped that his suggestion to form a yachtsmen's study circle for the winter months would have proved as popular as it did. The magazine's editor, Maurice Griffiths, published the letter and, on 5 November, 27 cruising yachtsmen met at a restaurant on Charing Cross Road. Thus was the Little Ship Club formed to give sailors something to do over the winter. An informal dinner was planned for 1 December and it was suggested that the meal be reminiscent of summer cruises. 'Chops, chips, bread, cheese and pint of beer' appeared on the suggested menu.

Each passing year saw the club increase in popularity, and 530 members and guests attended the annual dinner in 1937. Those who joined were not the super-rich who had immaculate yachts with large crews and competed in the smart regattas; instead they were those who sailed all manner of small boats for the sheer pleasure of doing so – and that philosophy still draws members to the clubhouse on the banks of the Thames in the City of London.

QUOTES ON BOATS

Loose lips sink ships.
World War II poster slogan

SAIL REPAIR KIT

Here's what you should have on board to cope with most emergencies

Palm: a leather cover for your thumb and palm that allows you to drive needles through thick sailcloth.

Tools: scissors, pliers, hammer, grommets and punches, Stanley knife, disposable lighter.

Needles: smear with Vaseline and keep in an airtight container to prevent rust.

Thread and twine: carry different weights and grades of sailmakers' thread and whipping twine.

Sticky-back Dacron: can be used as a short-term repair.

Sailcloth: assorted sizes and weights.

Sail slides: losing a slide is likely to cause further sail failure.

Webbing: to reinforce repairs.

Tape: you can never have too much tape.

The sheet bend

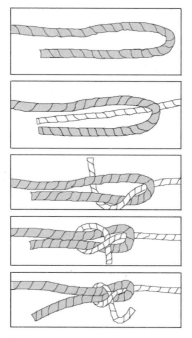

Take the end of two ropes and make a bight (open loop) in the thicker rope. Pass the thinner rope through the bight then around and under it. Loop the thinner rope over the thicker part then under its own standing part. Pull tight and check that loose ends are both on the same side.

WORDS ON THE WATER

How happy is the sailor's life,
From coast to coast to roam;
In every port he finds a wife,
In every land a home.
Isaac Bickerstaff, *Thomas and Sally*

WHAT'S THE BOTTOM LIKE?

Types of seabed as found on United Kingdom Hydrographic Office charts:

Algae • Basalt • Boulders
Cinders • Clay • Cobbles
Coral • Diatoms • Foram inifera
Glauconite • Gravel • Ground
Kelp • Lava • Madrepore
Manganese • Marl • Mussels
Mud • Ooze • Oysters
Pebbles • Polyzoa • Pteropods
Pumice • Quartz • Radiolaria
Rock • Sandwaves • Sand
Scoriae • Shells • Shingle
Silt • Spring in seabed • Sponge
Stones • Tufa • Weed

SEA SAYINGS

Taken aback/take the wind out of your sails

A sudden shift of wind or slip in the helmsman's concentration can lead to the wind blowing on the wrong side of a warship's sails, putting massive pressure on rigging and masts and making the ship unsteady. This unwelcome situation was always unexpected and could take the wind out of your sails, quite literally.

GOTCHA!

Yachting can have a reputation for stuffiness, which is largely undeserved. In fact that act of spending your wages on becoming wet and uncomfortable is surely evidence of a healthy sense of humour. This yachting wit is tested on occasion by the yachting press and *Yachting Monthly* in particular. It's certainly not an annual occurrence, but the April issue of this venerable organ often contains a story that should be taken with a pinch of sea salt. News of a revolutionary floating anchor was met with astonishment by some, but wry smiles by the more astute. Sailors on the River Hamble were in uproar about plans for a Sail-thru McDonald's, as were yachtsmen in both Jersey and Guernsey when informed that the bridge to be built between the two islands would curtail their cruising. Dogs that could sniff out woodworm were considered a good thing, however, and it was hoped that they would also be able to detect the dreaded polyestermite that allegedly chews through fibreglass boats.

THE BIRTH OF THE OUTBOARD

Legend has it that the modern outboard engine came to exist because an American engineer had almost fainted after rowing across Lake Okauchee in Wisconsin to fetch an ice cream for a lady friend. That was in 1906 and the name of that man, Ole Evinrude, is still well-known among outboard users today. In fact Evinrude was not the first, although he is the only one of the pioneers whose name is still known. The way had been prepared for Evinrude's success by men such as T Reece of Philadelphia, who patented a screw propeller that was driven by hand. Attached by screw clamps, it could be moved from one boat to another and so in many ways was the forerunner of the modern outboard. Variations on Reece's theme followed but it was a Frenchman named Trouvé who in 1888 claimed to have invented the first motorised outboard. His machine was driven by electricity; it was not until 1896 that the American Motors Company produced a petrol-powered version. Evinrude's outboard followed a decade later and could develop 1.5hp via its horizontal cylinder, vertical crankshaft and underwater gear housing. The rest is outboard history.

QUOTES ON BOATS

Any fool can carry on, but a wise man knows how to shorten sail in time.
Joseph Conrad, novelist

WHAT TO DO IF YOU COME ACROSS A MINE

1. Do not shoot at it. You may think that a shot from a rifle at a safe distance may set off the mine and thus remove the danger. However it is possible for the bullet to pierce the mine without triggering the detonator. The mine may then sink and be washed ashore in a dangerous state.

2. Do not try and tow it to port. Obvious, really.

3. Note the time and your position and report the sighting to the naval authorities via the Coastguard. Broadcast on Channel 16 so that other shipping in the vicinity is aware.

4. The Annual Summary of Admiralty Notices to Mariners contains information for fishermen who are unlucky enough to pick up a mine in their nets.

Huckleberry Finn and his friends were beginning to wish that they had stayed at home to paint the picket fence after all.

WHICH WAY'S UP?

Nothing at sea is a simple as it first appears. Take directions for example: as well as port and starboard replacing left and right there is also the concept of leeward (away from the wind) and windward (towards it). Port and starboard are relative to the direction of the vessel, while leeward and windward depend on the direction of the wind. At least compass directions, such as North, remain constant and uncomplicated – if only.

Direction can be referenced to three different Norths and if you confuse them you could easily find yourself on the rocks.

True North is measured from the Geographic North Pole – the place where explorers stick their flags. Magnetic North is measured from the Magnetic North Pole – which does not coincide with the Geographic North and can move about. Compass North is wherever the north-seeking end of the compass needle says it is. This can be affected by all manner of metallic and electrical objects on board.

Charts normally show True North, but bearings and tracks calculated from this must be converted to Magnetic before being used to steer by.

FIRE!

Fire and boats do not mix. There are, of course, large amounts of water available to put out the fire, but by the time you've thrown a bucket over the side, hauled it on board and thrown it on to the inferno, the flames may have got the upper hand. Fire was a constant hazard on naval sailing ships and in 1568 an order was given to the entire British fleet regarding measures that should be put in place so that fires could be quickly extinguished.

The captain was to order that two large casks be cut in half and chained securely. 'The soldiers and mariners to piss in them that they may always be full of urine to quench fire work with, and two or three pieces of old sail ready to wet the piss; and always cast it on the fire work as need shall require.' Effective though it was, modern mariners now use fire extinguishers instead.

HOW TO ABANDON SHIP

A few points to remember if you need to take to your life raft

Abandon ship only as a last resort.
If you have time, take extra food, water and distress equipment.
Attach the raft's painter to the yacht before launching it.
Put the fittest and strongest person on board first to help others in.
Cut yourself free of the yacht only if there is a risk of its sinking – it is a bigger target for rescuers to find.
Take seasickness tablets – being sick will weaken you.
Do not drink seawater or urine.

THE REALITY OF SAILING

Chopping onions

Hot food makes for a happy crew and many seaworthy stews, curries and casseroles start with the chopping of an onion. Not a difficult task you may think, but try doing it when your world is at a 30 degree angle and the worktop keeps pitching up and down. There is no way that the onions will stay on the chopping board at such an angle, so you must find a way of getting everything level.

The best solution is to sit on the floor and jam yourself against something solid. The board can then be wedged between your knees and your chest allowing one hand to hold the onion (or whatever else requires chopping) and one hand to wield the knife. You can rock your body forward and backwards and from side to side to counter the movement of the boat and keep everything on an even keel. So much for the romance of sail.

Millions of years ago that ammonites (those curly fossils) appeared in the 143
Earth's seas

NAUTICAL PUZZLES

Where can you sail no lower yet float no higher?
Answer on page 153

WORDS ON THE WATER

The Lord is my pilot, I shall not drift.
He guides me across the dark waters.
He steers me in deep channels.
He keeps my log.
He pilots me by the star of holiness for His name's sake.
Yea, though I sail 'mid the fenders and tempests of life I shall dread
no danger for He is near me.
His love and care shelter me.
He prepares a harbour before me in the homeland of eternity.
He anoints the waves with oil, my ship rides calmly.
Surely sunlight and starlight shall favour me on my voyages and I will
rest in the port of our Lord forever.

Captain John H Roberts, 1874

QUOTES ON BOATS

Raise your sail one foot and you get 10 feet of wind
Chinese proverb

WHO'S BEEN TELLING TALES?

Non-sailors watch with awe as the yachtsman pulls in one rope, lets
out another, sucks his teeth, glances aloft and then declares the sails
are properly set. It may seem like dark magic, but the basic techniques
of sail trim are surprisingly easy as long as the sails are fitted with telltales. These strands of wool or sailcloth are attached to specific parts
of the mainsail and genoa (the large triangular front sail) and indicate
how the wind is flowing over them. If they fly horizontally with little
fluttering you know that you are doing something right – if not then
you'll need to pull in or let out a sheet, change the boat's angle to the
wind, or adjust one of the other lines that controls the sail's shape.

Sailing by the genoa telltales is perhaps easiest of all. Take the
helm in one hand and sit on the leeward side of the boat. Fix the
genoa telltales with a beady eye and watch what they are doing. If
the telltales on the windward side of the sail start to lift, then steer
away from the wind; if the ones on the other side lift, then steer
towards the wind. If both sides are flying straight and true then do
nothing. Simple!

For use at sea in the event of radio failure

Message understood

 or or

Drop a message   Rocking wings   Flash landing or
                                            navigation lights
                                            twice

Message not understood – repeat

 or

Straight and level flight   Circling

Sequence of three manoeuvres meaning proceed in this direction

1. Circle vessel at least once
2. Cross low ahead of vessel, rocking winds
3. Overfly vessel and head in required direction

Your assistance is no longer required

Cross low astern of vessel, rocking wings

*Note: if necessary, engine pitch or volume may be
varied as an alternative to rocking wings*

Height, in feet, of the mast of Cheyenne, the world-record-breaking catamaran 145

Prince Albert liked his new pipe enormously,
though smoking it always made his eyes water.

WORDS ON THE WATER

Captain Joshua Slocum, the first man to sail around the world
single-handed, had some words of advice after completing his epic
journey in 1898.

To succeed, however, in anything at all, one should go
understandingly about his work and be prepared for every
emergency. I see, as I look back over my own small achievements,
a kit of not too elaborate carpenters' tools, a tin clock, and some
carpet-tacks, not a great many, to facilitate the enterprise as
already mentioned in the story. But above all to be taken into
account were some years of schooling, where I studied with
diligence Neptune's laws, and these laws I tried to obey when I
sailed overseas; it was worth the while.

Captain Joshua Slocum, *Sailing Alone Around the World*

NELSON'S PRAYER

On the morning of 21 October 1805, with the combined fleets of France and Spain then in sight, Nelson wrote this prayer in his diary:

May the great God, whom I worship, grant to my Country and for the benefit of Europe in general, a great and glorious Victory: and may no misconduct, in any one, tarnish it: and may humanity after victory be the predominant feature in the British Fleet.

For myself individually, I commit my life to Him who made me and may His blessing light upon my endeavours for serving my Country faithfully.

To him I resign myself and the just cause which is entrusted to me to defend.

Amen. Amen. Amen.

Before the battle commenced he ordered for the famous signal to be raised: 'England expects every man to do his duty.' By four o'clock that afternoon Nelson was dead.

NAUTICAL PUZZLES

What lies on the bottom of the ocean and twitches?
Answer on page 153

SOUNDS AT SEA

Sound signals used when vessels are in sight of one another

One short blast
I am altering my course to starboard

Two short blasts
I am altering my course to port

Three short blasts
My engines are going astern

Five short blasts
I am unsure of your intentions

Four short blasts followed by one short blast
I intend to turn completely around to starboard

Four short blasts then two short
I intend to turn completely around to port

Two long blasts followed by one short blast
I wish to overtake you on your starboard side

Two long blasts followed by two short blasts
I wish to overtake you on your port side

One long blast, one short blast, one long blast, one short blast
You may overtake me on the side indicated

THE MARY ROSE

The Mary Rose is the only six-teenth century warship on display anywhere in the world. Built between 1509 and 1511, she was one of the first ships able to fire a broadside, and was a firm favourite of King Henry VIII. The Mary Rose had a keel length of 32m and a breadth of 11.66m. Her length at the waterline is estimated to have been 38.5m and her draught 4.6m. After a long and successful career, she sank accidentally during an engagement with the French fleet in 1545. Her rediscovery and raising were seminal events in the history of nautical archaeology.

The search for and discovery of the Mary Rose was a result of the dedication of one man, the late Alexander McKee. In 1965, in conjunction with the Southsea branch of the British Sub-Aqua Club, he initiated project Solent Ships. While on paper this was a plan to examine a number of known wrecks in the Solent, Alex McKee really hoped to find the Mary Rose. He succeeded in 1967, and the Mary Rose was placed on a special cradle and lifted from the seabed in 1982. After painstaking restoration work she was put on display in Portsmouth.

QUOTES ON BOATS

When men come to like a sea life, they are not fit to live on land.
Dr Samuel Johnson, scholar

MEET THE CAT

The Cat may not be the most imaginatively named catamaran in the world, but when you're as big and fast as she is, you can call yourself whatever you want. She's the fastest car ferry in North America and if you're sailing on the waters between Canada and the US you had better watch out. The Cat can only carry 250 cars, but she does so at incredible speed. Once in open water The Cat can accelerate to 48 knots in less than a minute and makes the passage from Maine to Nova Scotia in less than three hours. Conventional ferries take six hours to make the crossing. The Cat is driven by twin 19,000hp engines, which drive pumps that blast out jets of water from the stern, pushing the wave-piercing bows through the sea. Each jet expels a remarkable 18,000 litres of water per second. The exceptional speed of The Cat is a result of the vessel's aluminium construction – she's 91m long and 21m wide but weighs in at just 300 tonnes. Most remarkable of all on this monster cat is the wheel with which the captain steers her – it's just 16cm in circumference.

The clove hitch

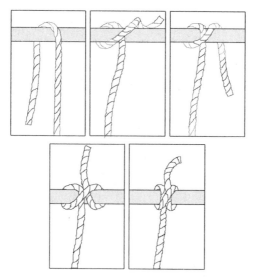

Pass a length of rope around the object (such as a spar) and then over again, crossing the working end of the rope over its standing part. Keeping the rope parallel to the first turn, tuck the working end underneath the second turn. Pull on both ends to tighten.

WORDS ON THE WATER

Few sailors can behold the ship in which they have sailed sinking before their eyes without the same emotion of distress and pity almost which the spectacle of a drowning man excites in them. She has grown a familiar name; a familiar object; thus far she had borne them in safety; she has been rudely beaten, and yet has done her duty; but the tempest has broken her down at last; all the beauty is shorn from her; she is weary with the long and dreadful struggle with the vast forces that Nature arrayed against her; she sinks, a desolate, abandoned thing in mid-ocean, carrying with her a thousand memories, which surge up in the heart with the pain of a strong man's tears.

William Clark Russell, *The Wreck of the Grosvenor*

SAILING STEREOTYPES

The grown-up dinghy racer

They may be in their mid-thirties but the Grown-Up Dinghy Racer (GUDR) is attempting to keep the years at bay by continuing to sail dinghies long after the other grown-ups have moved on to sailing vessels that have a fridge and a toilet. They take everything rather seriously and only take to the water to race. They drive an estate car, but are quick to point out that it's a sporty estate (that came with their sales manager's job). They like to do things properly and have only a rough comprehension of sportsmanship. For the GUDR, rules are all-important. They'd rather lose the race but win the protest afterwards. The changing rooms are their favourite domain where they like to walk around naked for as long as possible, addressing people by the surname with an 'o' or 'y' added to the end to show that they are sporty. They are likely to have attractive yet dull girlfriends whom they bore with blow-by-blow accounts of each race. GUDRs are likely to go on to to become pushy Dinghy Dads.

WATCH UP, DOC?

Time	Name	Abbreviated name
0001-0400	Middle Watch	Middle (Hey Diddle Diddle)
0400-0800	Morning Watch	The Morning
0800-1200	Forenoon Watch	The Forenoon
1200-1600	Afternoon Watch	The Afternoon
1600-1800	First Dog Watch	First Dog
1800-2000	Last Dog	Last Dog
2000-0001	First Watch	The First (Geoff Hurst)
All Night in Bed	'All Night in'	(Rin Tin Tin)

EVER THE OPTIMIST

It may look like a bathtub with a mast, but the Optimist dinghy forms the bedrock of worldwide sailing. Designer Clark Mills built the first Oppy (as they are affectionately known) in 1947. More than a quarter of a million have been built since and Optimists remain the most popular way for young people to get afloat. Oppies are sailed in over 110 countries by over 150,000 young people and it is the only dinghy approved by the International Sailing Federation exclusively for sailors under 16 years of age. Over 60% of the skippers at the 2004 Athens Olympics were former Optimist sailors and over 50% of the medal-winning skippers competed at Optimist International Championships.

---

150 *Speed, in kilometres, that can be reached by ice sailors standing on skates within a wingsail*

DURING THE COMPILATION OF THIS BOOK,
THE COMPANION TEAM...

Went sailing 47 times, and ran aground twice

Lost three wellies to the mud

Discovered the impenetrable world of nautical nomenclature

Resolved to pack in work, sell the house and sail to somewhere sunny twice daily

Thought to put on their oilies only after the skies had opened up on at least five occasions

Reminded themselves that a bad day afloat beats a good day in the office

Prepared and ate 36 ham and salad rolls, 14 of which were soggy

Spent 13 hours practising knots

Remembered leaky heads and fiddling about with impellers and forgot the plans to sail into the sunset

Wondered if there could be really be a need for quite so many knots

Compiled 89 jokes about seamen, 21 of which were of negligible comic value, and none of which are printable here

Drank 270 cups of tea, of which 18 were made with UHT milk, and three of which were knocked over during accidental gybes

Imbibed 14 pints of Guinness at the London boat show

Abandoned ship

Please note that although every effort has been made to ensure accuracy in this book, the above statistics may be the result of waterlogged minds; take them with a pinch of salt

The cure for anything is salt water:
sweat, tears or the sea.
Isak Dinesen, author

The answers. As if you needed them.

P13. First, fill up the three-litre jug. Pour the three litres into the five-litre container. Refill the three-litre jug and once again pour it into the five-litre container until it is full. The three-litre jug now contains one litre. Empty the five-litre container back into the storage tank and then pour the one litre of diesel into it. Now, fill the three-litre jug up again and pour it into the yachtsman's five-litre container. The container will now contain the desired four litres.

P20. 112 – two sides will need 29 nails each, the other two sides only 27 nails each, as the nails in the corners double up.

P27. Clare Francis, who was sponsored by Robertsons Jam in the days when the company used the golliwog logo. Her yacht was named Robertson's Golly.

P37. Your temper.

P48. You sail a lilac yacht with a keel from Denmark (probably). If you don't, you don't think like the rest of us.

P53. Fill the sink and then let the water drain out. If the water circulates anticlockwise then you're in the Northern Hemisphere; if it goes out in a clockwise swirl then you're in the Southern Hemisphere.

P60. Pungy – the Pungy is a type of schooner from Chesapeake Bay, where it was used for dredging oysters. The others are canoes common to the Micronesian Islands and Malay Archipelago.

P68. Man overboard.

P75. Two hours – 26/ (7+6).

P84. Sixty-six feet. One half (three-sixths) is in the ground, one third (two-sixths) is underwater, which leaves one-sixth, which measures 11 feet. If one-sixth equals 11 feet, six-sixths equals 66 feet.

P94. All hands on deck.

P104. Women and children first.

P107. The seven seas.

P114. Either – any port in a storm!

P128. Vice Admiral Horatio Lord Nelson – the half-nelson is a wrestling hold in which the wrestler puts an arms under an opponent's arm and exerts pressure on the back of the neck.

P131. Because the sea weed.

P144. On the Dead Sea. It is lowest point on the Earth's surface, some 400m below actual sea level, yet its high salinity makes it incredibly buoyant.

P147. A nervous wreck.

FURTHER READING

The Mariners Handbook,
RO Morris, Hydrographer of the Navy

The Guinness Book of Ships and Shipping, Tom Hartman

Sailing, a beginner's guide, David Seidman

Yachting World Handboook, D Phillips-Birt

Boat Data Book, Ian Nicolson

Reed's Skipper's Handbook, Malcolm Pearson

Salty Dog Talk, Bill Beavis and Richard McCloskey

The Illustrated Encyclopaedia of Ships and Boats,
Graham Blackburn

The Yachtsman's Week-end Book,
John Irving, Douglas Service & Douglas Phillips-Birt

The Yachtsman's and Boatowner's Handbook,
Richard Beaumont

Blue Water Countdown, Geoff Pack

The Impossible Voyage, Chay Blythe

Sailpower, Peter Nielsen

Yachtsman's Ten Language Dictionary,
Barbara Webb & Michael Manton

He who goes to sea for pleasure would go to hell to pass the time!

Anon

ACKNOWLEDGEMENTS

We gratefully acknowledge permission to reprint extracts of copyright material in the book from the following authors, publishers and executors:

117 Days Adrift by Maurice and Marilyn Bailey reproduced by permission of the publishers A & C Black Publishers Ltd.

Come Wind or Weather by Clare Francis reproduced by kind permission of John Johnson, Author's Agent.

Reprinted with permission of Scribner, an imprint of Simon and Schuster Adult Publishing Group, from *The Old Man and the Sea* by Ernest Hemingway, Copyright 1952 by Ernest Hemingway. Copyright renewed © 1980 by Mary Hemingway.

Come Aboard by Eric Hiscock reproduced by permission of the publishers, A & C Black.

Cape Horn – The Logical Route by Bernard Moitessier reproduced by permission of Sheridan House Inc.

The Odyssey by Homer and translated by E. V. Rieu, revised translation by D. C. H. Rieu, Penguin Classics 1946, revised translation 1991. Copyright 1946 by E. V. Rieu. Revised translation copyright © Estate of the late E. V. Rieu, and D. C. H. Rieu, 1991, 2003. Reproduced by permission of Penguin Books Ltd.

INDEX

FILL YOUR BOOKSHELF AND YOUR MIND

The Birdwatcher's Companion Twitchers, birders, ornithologists and garden-tickers: there are many species of birdwatcher, and you're all catered for by this unique book. ISBN 9781861058331

The Cook's Companion Whether your taste is for foie gras or fry-ups, this tasty compilation is an essential ingredient in any kitchen, boiling over with foodie fact and fiction. ISBN 9781861057723

The Gardener's Companion For anyone who has ever put on a pair of gloves, picked up a spade and gone out into the garden in search of flowers, beauty and inspiration. ISBN 9781861057716

The Golfer's Companion Bogeys and shanking, plus fours and six irons, the alleged etiquette of caddies – all you need to know about the heaven and hell of golf is in this unique book. ISBN 9781861058348

The Ideas Companion This fascinating book tells the stories behind the trademarks, inventions, and brands that we come across every day. ISBN 9781861058355

The Legal Companion From lawmakers to lawbreakers, this fascinating compilation offers a view of the oddities, quirks, origins and stories behind the legal world. ISBN 9781861058386

The Literary Companion Whether your Dickens is Charles or Monica, your Stein Gertrude or Franken, here's your book. Literary fact and fiction from Rebecca East to Vita Sackville-West. ISBN 9781861057983

The London Companion From Edgware to Morden, Upminster to Ealing, here's your chance to explore the history and mystery of the most exciting capital city in the world. ISBN 9781861057990

The Moviegoer's Companion Explore the strange and wonderful world of movies, actors, cinemas and salty popcorn in all their glamorous glory from film noir to Matt LeBlanc. ISBN 9781861057976

The Politics Companion The history, myths, great leaders and greater liars of international politics are all gathered around the hustings in this remarkable compilation. ISBN 9781861057969

The Sailing Companion This is the book for everyone who knows their starboard from their stinkpot, and their Raggie from their stern – and anybody who wants to find out. ISBN 9781861058393

The Traveller's Companion For anyone who's ever stared at a distant plane, wondered where its going, and spent the rest of the day dreaming of faraway lands. ISBN 9781861057730

The Walker's Companion If you've ever laced a sturdy boot, packed a cheese sandwich, and stepped out in search of stimulation and contemplation, then this book is for you. ISBN 9781861058256

The Wildlife Companion Animal amazements, ornithological oddities and botanical beauties abound in this compilation of natural need-to-knows and nonsense for wildlife-lovers. ISBN 9781861057709